PATRICK
MILWAUKEE, WISCONSIN 53222

P9-DCX-246

WITHDRAWN

WHY THINGS GO WRONG

PATRICK & BEATRICE HAGGERTY LIBRARY
MOUNT MARY COLLEGE
MILWAUKEE, WISCONSIN 53222

WHY THINGS GO WRONG

Deming Philosophy in a Dozen Ten-Minute Sessions

GARY FELLERS

PELICAN PUBLISHING COMPANY
Gretna 1994

Copyright © 1994
By Gary Fellers
All rights reserved

The word "Pelican" and the depiction of a pelican are trademarks of Pelican Publishing Company, Inc., and are registered in the U.S. Patent and Trademark Office.

Library of Congress Cataloging-in-Publication Data
Fellers, Gary, 1951-
    Why things go wrong : Deming philosophy in a dozen ten-minute sessions / Gary Fellers.
        p. cm.
    Includes bibliographical references.
    ISBN 1-56554-070-0
    1. Deming, W. Edwards (William Edwards), 1900- —Contributions in management. 2. Management. I. Title.
    HD38.D439 F45   1994
    658—dc20
                                                          94-4769
                                                          CIP

Manufactured in the United States of America

Published by Pelican Publishing Company, Inc.
1101 Monroe Street, Gretna, Louisiana 70053

Contents

58.4
318
994

Acknowledgments

The perceptive people listed below gleaned the wisdom of the ages and shared it with me as we developed this book. It would have been impossible to write a bad or irrelevant manuscript with their help. To protect my reviewers, I must say that all the jokes are mine. Unless stated otherwise, the amusing case studies involved me. I was always the good guy.

Ken Blanchard—Coauthor of *The One Minute Manager*

Richard Lawson—TQM Coordinator, DSM Chemicals

Ted Kinni—Writer, The Business Reader

Jenny McAlister—Housewife

Dr. Joe Tiller—Psychologist and School Administrator

Mike Gautney—Human Resources Manager, Weyerhaeuser

John Kroll—Writer and Editor, Fox Broadcasting Company

Jenny Tokash—Quality Assurance Manager, Carborundum Company

Rick Bruce—Quality Technician, Cryovac Company, Simpsonville, South Carolina

LaVerne Johnson—President, International Institute of Learning-New York

Charles Givens—Best-selling author of *SuperSelf* and others

Dr. Mike McDonald—Professor, Georgia Southern University

Dr. Nabil Ibrahim—Professor, Augusta College

Mike Henderson—Plant Manager, Cedar Rapids, Iowa

Kevin O'Gorman—Manufacturing General Manager, Carborundum Company

Mary DeZurik—Bookstore Manager, Greenville, South Carolina

I owe the most to Dr. W. Edwards Deming. His theories hold this book together. My wife, Pam Fellers, provides constant inspiration for many reasons, not the least of which is her good looks. My parents, George and Jackie Fellers, made me curious. Nina Kooij and Dr. Milburn Calhoun of Pelican Publishing Company discovered this book. Christine Benson turned an engineer's sloppy writing into something an English major would be proud to claim.

Purpose of This Condensed Book: Not Just Another Deming Text

"How do we get management to change?" is the most frequently asked question I have to ponder. The people at the top have many conflicting issues to balance. It takes a convincing and tactful message to get onto their "mental agendas." So I wrote this book. I condensed it so busy executives can read it in short spurts. I included no cheap shots toward management—an easy-to-target group who cannot defend themselves against a tactless writer with a sharp pencil. You can lend them your copy and not fear the ax—or the nuances of cunning bureaucrats.

Time is your most important asset. If something powerful has already motivated you to read this book, you may skip ahead to chapter 1 if you're in a hurry. Otherwise, keep reading. I'll capture your interest within two minutes. An insightful old-timer told me once that good and bad managers are ninety-five percent the same, but differ in all-important aspects. This book is about that five percent where they differ. I included very few evident remarks and platitudes. We all know, for example, that the golden rule will take you a long way in life. I do not bother to tell you such obvious things again.

I heard Charles Givens say once, "Doing more of what doesn't work won't make it work any better." This book is for those folks who believe there may be another recipe. Just working harder is seldom the complete answer. Discover why many firms have found themselves having to re-engineer—to constructively downsize.

Things go wrong in business because we make many decisions with fear, politics, lack of knowledge, and personal agendas lurking just beneath the surface. These problems are like cutoff tree trunks in a lake. The stumps are under the water ready to wreck the boat at any moment. The water level rises and falls uncontrollably as a result of economic conditions and uncertainty within the firm. Instead of eliminating the stumps, we often just try raising the water level a little to buy some time. As a result, the larger good of both the firm and its employees often suffers when we eliminate symptoms—not the causes behind *why* things go wrong.

This isn't a management-bashing book. For at least five years, the comment "Management isn't interested in quality" has not been true. A more appropriate and understandable comment would be: Executives aren't inquisitive about inefficient (or ineffective) approaches to improvement, or making changes that would risk their careers if they fail to meet short-term financial expectations. Who would expect otherwise? This condensed book is about "having your cake and eating it too"—something that isn't easy. As Peter Drucker said, "Sooner or later, everything degenerates to work." The how-to guidelines are for those who aren't content to just go through the motions of the latest "management fix," but who want to see improved financial performance, with fate on their side. Luck frequently visits the prepared mind. This quick-read will prepare yours. Unlike when reading some longer books about Deming, you won't have time to forget chapter 1 before you finish the last section. You'll finally see how the pieces fit together. When this happens, synergy erupts (2+2=5) if you act on what you learn.

Dr. W. Edwards Deming was the management guru who taught the U.S. automakers how to compete in the 1980s. He developed a process for bringing about long-lasting improvements: It calls for "removing some stumps" and explains *why* things go wrong. Unlike some academic theorists, Dr. Deming showed how to prevent many of the problems. Traditional managers often create new job positions or bureaucratic procedures to endure or to cover up problems. Deming's concepts, however, involve eliminating the root causes. No other expert provides a universal theory of management like this— there are no bandaids, only preventative solutions. Companies that have implemented his system can attest to the benefits it brought about. But for the Deming transformation truly to work, both the top executives who set the long-range course of the company and the folks way down in the trenches who do the work must comprehend the basic workings of the new approach. Often, neither of the two extremes understands— and for the same reason: They have no time to attend seminars or to read tedious books. That's why I wrote this primer.

At most firms the Deming transition starts in the middle of the organization and slowly diffuses upward and downward. This works okay in some instances, but now it is also time to "light the candle at both ends." The two extremes of the spectrum, upper managers and frontline employees, need a stripped-down explanation of Deming's principles they can easily comprehend during a single round-trip flight or over a dozen ten-minute breaks.

Quality-minded change agents who need a quick way of enlightening upper management will treasure this book. The language ridicules no one, and thus will not get you into trouble. Top executives often want a preview of a recommended book, whether it is for themselves or the frontline employees—the ones who want "out of the dark" as management changes its ways of doing business. Management has to implement the philosophy, but the "doers in the trenches" want to know the reasons why things change and what it will mean to them. Others will also benefit, such as administrative and service managers who have often shunned the longer, more technical books on the Deming philosophy.

Most quality managers, consultants, and statistical trainers know something about the Deming philosophy by now, but I have found that others generally have not had the several hundred hours it takes to grasp the material. This short, two-hour guidebook can benefit these employees to whom the internal trainers often have limited access. It can also help the previously informed group formulate a nonmathematical way of explaining Deming to other managers—the first book to provide this.

How did I come to the realization that the earlier books missed some key people like upper managers who could have facilitated the change, or in some cases prevented failure?

First: In my travels, I frequently talk to executives on airplanes. I found a significant number who could not tell me what they meant when they said, "We are implementing the Deming philosophy." They had companies to run and had lacked the time to assimilate Dr. Deming's ideas—concepts that reverse a large part of traditional managerial practices.

Second: Many executives told me they were part of a "Deming" company. Yet I knew from consulting there or by talking with friends who worked there that their firms had almost all of the **deadly diseases,** such as ruling by fear or managing by after-the-fact appraisals. Both are opposites of Deming's approach.

Third: At times others told me their firms had implemented the Deming philosophy but had witnessed no improvement in the bottom line. They missed the 2+2=5 synergy by not seeing how the pieces fit together. They failed to see *why things go wrong*. I have found that a total execution of Dr. Deming's theory yields an eventual, attributable bottom-line improvement of fifteen to seventy-five percent. (About twenty-five percent is typical.)

Fourth: Various executives told me they selected parts of *all* the experts' theories to form a new, composite approach for their company. This statement often means they learned a few scattered ideas and "cherry picked" the ones neatly fitting their existing management practices. I understand why this happens. We all like to confirm our private thoughts. I'm not saying Deming was the only guru who had something to say. They all have valuable insights, but Dr. Deming was the only one who gave us a new theory of management—one that can restore creativity and enthusiasm we too often lack.

Fifth: I have seen eyes glaze over as seminar attendees tuned out. When you say "Deming" to many frontline employees, they think to themselves, "Oh, no. Here comes another program. It will pass." If implemented correctly, it won't pass. The firm can never go back, nor will its employees want to. From the beginning, by reading this primer, the people in the trenches can understand why the transformation is necessary. Then they will want to help it move forward.

To keep this book short, I assume the success of other firms persuaded you of the need to consider change—there is no preaching provided here. I also assume you know that Dr. Deming made a profound impact on business efficiency throughout the world—he already established his credibility. I provide no lengthy case studies to convince you this is "the way to go because others did it." Nor do I include rigorous statistical explanations about the validity of Dr. Deming's theory. Because others have accomplished this well, I included a few references. In these few pages, I quickly lay the concepts out on the table, with recommendations for getting started. You decide if you want to do it. The Deming philosophy has been around for a while, and some of us have priceless, piercing experiences—ones I am about to share with you in a concise way. There are no benign doomsday alarms in this book to scold you. Others before you have experimented with ineffective approaches and witnessed the pain of disappointment. One thorn of experience—the learning from others—is worth a whole wilderness of warning.

Pay close attention to the *boldfaced, italicized* words. A new language of management is evolving around Deming's influence. You need to know these terms whether or not you adopt Dr. Deming's methods. As an example, throughout the book I use the word *frontline* to denote the fifty percent or so of the people who actually make the product, have contact with the customers, provide the direct service, or immediately aid those who do. These people could not go on vacation for three months if you wanted to stay in business. Clerical, hourly, or production operators aren't appropriate substitute terms for *frontline*. The frontline involves all these people as well as many salaried workers and managers.

Many firms have defined *empowerment* too narrowly—only involving people who physically touch the product or deal face-to-face with customers. We don't like to categorize this group; but when forced to, hourly, rank-and-file, production operators, or labor comes to mind. My definition of frontline broadens the scope to encompass these people and others. I see many forgotten and frustrated lower-tier (but not hourly) employees "in the trenches." Power has often moved from the front office straight to the rank-and-file while leaving out other important people who need more autonomy. I heard a department manager say, "If I die, I hope to be reincarnated as an hourly worker here. They're the only ones who are important." I do believe that the hourly employees (for lack of a better phrase) have many problem solutions—ones managers often do not have the foggiest idea of how to elicit. However, these frontline folks frequently need the forgotten, lower-level managers and engineers to hone and formalize their conclusions. Cast a wider net with your empowerment to include them also. I'll never forget when most of the managers in a nonunion papermill applied for the top production operator's hourly job. For them, the American dream of working like a dog for fifteen years or going to college to achieve respect and influence had died. I'm not talking about middle management at a far-away office, but *frontline,* indispensable employees near the point of manufacture or service.

It takes many months to achieve the Deming transition, but you can discover the basics in about two hours with this book. Here's what you must know before your firm begins the

Deming transition, and what you'll grasp from this reading:

1. Do we want to do this now?
2. How do we start?
3. What things will we eventually have to do, and in what order?
4. What resources will I need?
5. Who will the major players be?

A sixth question is equally important, but it arises only if your firm is near the middle of the transformation: Are we "really" there already, as people told me; or have we only allowed (or required) our employees to build a facade and pretend they made the transformation?

If you totally implement the Deming philosophy, you also accomplish the publicized *total quality management* (TQM) by hitting the problems "head-on"—conditions at the surface and issues deeply hidden in the status quo. And this pays big bucks. According to the December 1993 issue of *Quality* magazine, during the last five years, companies implementing *real* TQM created revenue increases almost twice that of the U.S. average, and with considerably fewer increases in employees. But beware: Deming and TQM are not interchangeable ideas. It is possible to execute someone's bureaucratic version of TQM without encountering the involved Deming topics, the ideas unenlightened management may not want to hear. A telltale clue one sees of an ineffective TQM "program" is that training (something easily acknowledged by management) took place, but there was no follow-up or implementation. I have found the flop to almost never be the fault of the TQM or quality facilitator, but other managers.

The predicament I see most often is management's essential personal agendas—*essential* implies "necessary to advance their careers." I am casting no blame. The presence of the ***deadly diseases*** of management—the crux of Deming's theory—doomed the TQM effort from day one. The standardized five-phase, TQM approach (discussed elsewhere) can work wonders, especially with larger firms that need some formality. But if you try to superimpose this system over the deadly diseases or in the absence of Deming's fourteen points—both subjects of this book—the returns will be unimpressive. With a stale TQM implementation, some improvements may come. However, profit-increasing opportunities remain. You will see a few low-hanging fruit. Lots of apples remain hidden in the tree.

Administration, service, and manufacturing get equal emphasis in this book as I show that at some point you have to say, "Enough theory, let's just *do* it." I guarantee you'll have the energy left and the motivation to *just do it* after reading this book. Isaac Newton said, "If I have been able to see farther than others, it was because I have stood on the shoulders of giants." Climb on for a better view, and let's get started.

Someone recently asked Dr. Deming what percentage of firms would be in the Deming mode in fifteen years. His answer: "All of them." This seemed bold and pompous at the time, but I finally understand. Those that do not manage according to his guidelines won't be here to compete. Granted, some will stumble into the Deming mode—not even knowing who he is—through mere trial and error and reflective common sense. Others will make it happen more quickly to prevent lost earnings now.

CHAPTER 1

What Are We Up to Here?

Deming and his influence emerged in this country at a desperate time when most American companies suffered pervasive quality problems. Other experts bombarded us from all sides with varied advice. As John Naisbitt stated, "We were drowning in information but starved for knowledge." Dr. Deming almost got lost in the crowd because we originally viewed him only as a person who wanted to sermonize about making extreme sacrifices to improve quality. Viewing him as the idealistic high priest of quality improvement, many production-oriented managers initially distanced themselves from Deming's philosophy. At the time, they thought quality was incompatible with production quantity, and their employers judged them by volume.

Two issues come to mind here. First—and we all know this now—improving quality through preventive measures always improves long-term profits, and usually daily production as well (market conditions prevailing). I have seen no exceptions to this statement in fifteen years of hands-on consulting. Second, Deming's concepts apply not just to quality but equally to production quantity, sales levels, service, employee satisfaction, and—to our delight—making money, both now and later. A decade of applications shows this. Remember the early misconceptions about quality-versus-quantity as you browse through this book and wonder why some firms were not quicker to embrace these concepts. These ideas seem obvious and clever today. Many of my client firms have more than a decade of experience with this Deming transition. I repeat what worked earlier for them and hope you learn from this secondhand knowledge. You don't have enough time to make all the same mistakes yourself.

A question to ponder as you read this book is why Deming spent so much time discussing what *not* to do. Part of the global predicament, in his opinion, was some of the old business-school teachings of decades past. These were counterproductive techniques designed with the intent of controlling people's behavior and thought processes to suit someone else's personal agenda—often relating to career management or ego nourishment, not lasting profitability. Peter Drucker said once that most of what we do as managers prevents someone from doing his job; and according to Deming, he was exactly right.

Part of the Deming transition you're about to learn involves relaxing some of the bureaucratic and autocratic management practices our professors taught us many years ago. Then, according to Deming, more creativity and synergy follow if we also pay attention to our goals and customers' needs. (Remember: The equation for synergy as the result of teamwork is 2+2=5.) With more creativity and synergy, we get an increased level of value-added behavior and a reduced level of teamwork-destroying internal competition. Further paybacks include less boss watching by the employees, and fewer personal agendas. Keep such payoffs in mind. These are the types of rewards Deming called the **unknowns and unknowables.** These things are ten times more important to profitability than any short-term accounting measure you can quantify. I have a list of *unknowns and unknowables* called the **intangibles:**

Creativity (looking for a better way)
Energy (self-motivated)
Inquisitiveness

Desire to work for the good of the team
Eagerness to compensate for co-workers' shortcomings
Willingness to achieve results that are necessary, but
   unnoticeable to the boss
Fervor for training others

Things go wrong when these intangibles aren't major corporate goals.

There are a few "unknowns and unknowables" that researchers squeezed out of the swamp through market research.

> A satisfied customer tells eight people. A dissatisfied one complains to over twenty.
>
> A satisfied car owner buys an average of four more over the next twelve years.
>
> Less than 4% of your dissatisfied customers bothers to tell you, but 91% never come back. (Customer-complaint data are tricky appraisal measures.)
>
> It costs five times as much to capture a new customer through advertising than it does to keep one through quality improvements.
>
> Multiply all internal cost-of-quality savings by ten— the stream of future new business will come. (*The Deming Vision,* page 72)

I need to upend another misconception. Contrary to what a few commentaries on his work state, Deming never said we don't need financial summaries to help guide us, nor did he maintain that accountants are injurious people. You'll find, however, that Deming despised the way we blindly "manage by exceptions," making belated attempts to control the business mostly by looking at the numbers, after the fact. I once heard him compare that to "driving your car by only looking in the rearview mirror."

The basic goal of the Deming philosophy is to get employees to "cast a wider net"—to be more creative and to search for more profitable ways of doing business. Because of the way we manage them, employees often "pull down the hatches" and carve out a comfortable and secure niche for themselves. It's their way of providing security for their families and preventing further "ego destruction." For them, it adds weight to their sense of place and belonging. You may say, "No, that's not true here." Would your employees let you know otherwise? In many firms, management practices have dampened, if not destroyed, much of the creative spirit.

Enough preaching! There is no more management-bashing in this book. We've had our fill of wrist slaps, when "attaboys" were frequently more appropriate. I often equate managers I have met over the last several decades to lion hunters. They hustle. (There are no lazy lion hunters.) In most cases, all that they needed was a new way of looking at things, not nasty criticism. Realizing this will open your mind to the rest of this book.

A hospital administrator summarized some of our problems when he said, "If you don't have the right road map, no amount of struggling will get you there." This book is your "right road map."

You'll get only a general knowledge of the theory here, with only few specifics. I would rather you be generally correct with the Deming theory than precisely wrong with another management view. Let's begin.

Deming said the most critical shortcoming of managers was their inability to understand variation. He meant that most, if not all, variation fits into one of two categories:

Common causes—These are elusive departures from the way we want things to be, deviations that the frontline employees can't control. These problems are usually interdepartmental, often political, and frequently accepted as "the nature of the beast." They seem to occur repeatedly by chance—like the spin of a roulette wheel.

Local faults—These are often mistakes the frontline workers can explain, and likely correct by themselves.

   It is important that you read that again.

   As you'll see, most variation results from ***common causes,*** those complex interdepartmental issues that the frontline employees can't presently resolve effectively. (The status quo often hides the root causes.) The emergence of common causes appears random, like drawing cards from a fair deck. Some days you just get a bad draw. The world is inherently uncertain, and people cannot control most of this variability through direct, short-term approaches. A simplistic example: As you leave for the doctor's office, your spouse says, "You've got to be back in two hours!" The common causes beyond your control include traffic, how many sick people are in line, how long the doctor has to attend to the patients ahead of you, and so forth.

   Another example: Assume it takes an average of six minutes to wait on a customer in a fast-food restaurant. At times the disparity is due to a ***local fault.*** In these cases, the server or local supervisor is accountable. Examples are daydreaming, the server's sloppiness, horseplay, or the manager's negligence about going to the bank for change, etc. If we are paying attention, we can usually identify and correct such problems.

   Consider the dozens of other perennial and elusive issues that create restaurant service-time problems:

> Equipment constantly breaking down
> Vendors sending the wrong supplies
> Late deliveries by vendors
> New-hires working by themselves without adequate training
> New faces behind the cash register every week
> Uncertainty in how many customers enter the door (Do tour buses call ahead?)
> Unpredictability in what the customers will order

When the frontline workers can't control these problems, we call them common causes because they are common to the system. Between eighty and ninety-five percent of all the problems firms face come from common causes and require that higher management solves them, or totally empowers someone else to do so. Sometimes the common cause variables randomly cancel each other. (For example, a vendor fails to deliver fish patties, but no one orders a fish sandwich.) Frequently, however, these variations don't neutralize each other, but compound and cause problems. Common causes are often unpredictable—like the spin of a roulette wheel.

To keep all the statistical graphs, bar charts, and calculations out of this simplified book, consider the following important mental demonstration. (You will need some way to explain this concept to executives who are impatient with the mathematics of the laws of chance.) Let me give you a glimpse of the end product of this visualization before I begin. Imagine a large, round table with a bull's-eye target painted on it. Sitting on top of the table in a bell-shapped stack are several thousand small blocks.

Now for the exercise: Envision painting a giant roulette wheel white so that you can write new numbers on it. In the case of the fast-food restaurant, assume we have on a page all the service-time data from a typical week. These data enable us to calculate an average time in line of six minutes and allow us to see how the variability away from this average occurred. Most service times will be near six: some sevens and fives (one away, plus or minus), a few eights and fours (two away), even fewer nines and threes, one or two 4.7s and 7.3s, and so forth. As you move away from the average of six minutes, the chances of occurrence diminish—slowly at first, then quickly. For a demonstration, we could simulate this situation with the painted roulette wheel. Let's mimic the statistical laws of chance (the common cause) for this restaurant. Write the observed week's individual service-time numbers onto the roulette-wheel positions: like 6.0, 6.1, 8.7, or 4.6 minutes. (Let this sink in for a minute: You write the observed data on the roulette wheel. A spin would yield a simulated future service time. And remember, this is a mental exercise. You will never actually have to do it.)

Another visual aid: Imagine like before the tabletop bull's-eye target. Now it is split in half with a dark line. In the bull's-eye center someone has written the number 6.0, representing the average of the observed service times. Moving out toward the right of the dark line, the next ring nearest the center contains a 6.1, the next a 6.2, then a 6.3, and so forth. Moving out from the left of the dark line, the centermost ring contains a 5.9 (one digit below the average). The outer rings at the edges of the table contain a 9.0 on the right and a 3.0 on the left, our extreme-most high and low service-time observations. Got the picture in your mind?

Third visual aid: We have several thousand one-inch blocks of wood that we will repeatedly place on the table in the appropriate rings of the target when that number occurs from the spin of the roulette wheel (simulating a customer service). We spin the roulette wheel several thousand times, on each occasion placing the wood blocks on the pertinent ring of the bull's-eye target on the table. Numbers above average go to the right; below average are placed to the left.

The mental exercise is over. Let this incubate for a few minutes as you envision the stack of blocks growing on the tabletop—from the results of the spins of the roulette wheel. Most will be near the bull's-eye center of six minutes.

Now, the relevant conclusions: Nature provided very organized laws of statistical chance. From spinning the roulette wheel, we'll eventually have a mound of blocks on the table that looks like a bell, with a peak in the center, slowly diminishing heights as we move away from the middle of the table, and almost no wood blocks near the edges. Mathematicians call this the *bell curve*—common language these days, even in the boardroom. We refer to creating the bell as the *roulette wheel* in this book. In a business setting, reference to the roulette wheel or the bell curve implies that the speaker has some knowledge of the unpredictable, but organized way things happen—from the dozens of elusive sources of common cause.

As a brief look ahead, the numbers on the roulette wheel could be any business variable. Examples include times required to process a purchase order, bookstore monthly sales figures, or weekly production data. Under the influence of our present management styles, the frontline workers can rarely change the odds—the numbers on the roulette wheel. Expecting them single-handedly to do so elicits many unexpected responses—all unprofitable. As Jacob Bronowski said, "Man masters nature not by force but by understanding." Nature provided the variation of the roulette wheel, thus some of the uncertainty of life. We must understand it.

Restaurant service-time variations falling away from the bull's-eye, but inside the bell, usually result from system common causes. There are many reasons for these aberrations, most of which are hard to pin down. On the other hand, an extreme block that fell off the table—an order that took longer than nine minutes or fewer than three minutes to fulfill—would probably be the result of local faults. The person on duty could identify and resolve the local faults. Of course, a service time faster than three minutes would not be a problem, but the same theory applies. In these cases, the server will know why service took less time than normal. (For example, maybe a gas line ruptured, authorities closed the road, and they were able to serve the day's three customers instantaneously.) At the good, left side of the table, there will be an occasional block near the edge—a 3.5 or 4.0 from the "spin of the roulette wheel." Everything was just right for that customer. She ordered something that was "up," she spoke clearly, there were no distractions, and she had the correct change. Can you see that the frontline workers cannot guarantee that this complex chain of events gets repeated for every customer? So it is a ridiculous comment for management to say, "I saw you serve that customer in 3.5 minutes. You did it once. Why can't you do it every time?" The roulette wheel doesn't work that way.

The ultimate shape of the bell curve doesn't tell the entire story. We need to know how the bell grew over time as we spun the roulette wheel—from a flat bell several inches high in the beginning, to one twenty or so inches tall later in the exercise. (In a business setting: How did the data occur over time?) If the bell grew fairly smoothly, with few stray peaks and valleys (with very few blocks ending up on the floor), the process is in *a state of statistical control,* or more simply, *in control.* Mathematicians would call this a *stable process,* whether it is good or bad. If the process is in control, the deviations from the average resulted mostly from *common causes* (system problems).

As a consultant, I have seen the following crux of the Deming theory demonstrated so many times it blows my mind:

> When you have a state of statistical control—meaning the deviations from the bull's-eye resulted from common causes—the issues to be addressed for the stable process are called *system problems.* For system problems the front-line workers are powerless to implement lasting solutions. They may have lots of ideas, but only higher management has the power, authority, and resources to eliminate these uncertainties. The reasons behind system problems are elusive and usually abundant. They often result from many confusing interactions among interdepartmental issues. The problems often evasively exist in the *white spaces* on the organization chart—not neatly within one department—and will require an *interdepartmental team* to solve.

Mathematically oriented trainers explain statistical control with charts, bar graphs, and computations—like the standard deviation. If you really need to know the math, see *SPC for Practitioners: Special Cases and Continuous Processes,* published by ASQC Quality Press in 1991. Someone in the company has to know the statistical manipulations. However, most folks can just forget the number crunching and move on. But reread the above extract.

Appendix A lists ideas on how to run interdepartmental

teams. Read it after examining this chapter. (I'll remind you.) For now, keep in mind that an interdepartmental team and a business meeting are not the same. Most firms have too many meetings, but not enough interdepartmental teams. Meetings are often pecking-order sparring matches, and/or unempowered. These difficulties are compounded by politics and bureaucracy—the two monsters that interdepartmental teams can slay. Teams must work on specific (and preferably self-imposed) issues. Rallying the troops to solve our system problems with no specific guidance on what monsters are banging at the door can be confusing. However, it is usually obvious what we need to correct. If there are not too many personal agendas, sometimes it is acceptable for supervisors to choose the problem. Examples of possible problems:

> Excessive time to process a customer complaint
> Internal scrap in department XYZ
> Excessive accidents
> Declining market share would be too broad—Try some-
>   thing related like:
>   Percent-on-time delivery problems
>   Field failure rate
>   In-process quality problem of a certain type
> And so forth

The whole idea behind the Deming philosophy is to crush system problems at their source, but we still need the teams. As we cure the diseases and implement the points, the only way I've seen to change the culture into a team orientation is through interdepartmental teams to solve existing system problems. You will learn best by positive examples. Solving decade-old problems gets people's attention. In five years, the synergies of Deming and the interdepartmental teams will be "business as usual," and no one will even talk about them.

Expecting someone to single-handedly prevent the random aberrations of the roulette wheel dooms this person to failure. There are jury rigs, however, that can make things look okay for a while. For example, milkshakes take extra time for the fast-food server. (I know, I used to work in fast food.) On a hectic day someone could lie and announce, "Sorry, no milk-shakes today, folks." Lost profits result.

I introduced the roulette wheel to give you a feel for the concept of statistical control and the bell curve. People who have taken a mathematical approach to understanding Deming will likely use those terms around you. The same math-oriented folks will likely use statistical process control (SPC) charts to contrast local faults with system problems. I chose to keep mathematical and graphic discussions out of this book because others have done that well. At a glance, you could see the analogy between the bell curve on the tabletop and the graphic approach. Now, consider the following for a less philo-sophical contrast of local faults and system problems:

Local Faults

- There is likely a short-term solution.
- Frontline employees are completely in control.
- The assignable cause is readily identifiable by frontline employees.
- The problem has become a good topic for the routine morning meeting.
- The old approach of "putting out fires" may work well.

As a culture, we are skillful at addressing local faults. When the "roulette comes off its hinges," we know how to get it reattached quickly.

System Problems

- These require long-term solutions. There is no quick-fix. We've tried lots of things with no "lasting" and efficient results. It keeps coming back!

- There is no single problem. There is a complex interaction of interdepartmental and interdisciplinary issues at work. No *one* person or department is responsible.

• Many issues often combine synergistically (2+2=5) to cause the evasive predicament. Looking for *the* problem will demoralize you. You will need to address many contributing factors simultaneously. We can't experience synergistic effects until all the pieces are in place. (Can you see why John Wayne types are having problems with the new approach? There's nothing to shoot or any one guy's butt to kick that will eradicate the problem. There are not many opportunities to be a hero and then ride off into the sunset. Those days are gone—except, of course, in a pure research lab or some start-up ventures.)

• System problems require a "different gear" than routine issues. For example, discussing tentative interdepartmental-team progress at routine business meetings can be counterproductive. We waste time getting ready for the meeting. How often have I heard: "We've got to get something done for this week's meeting. The boss will be there." Also, system problems take time. Many things are different with the Deming transition. This is one of them.

• The bureaucracy and politicians can't solve system problems; neither can unguided "professional career managers"—those whose single goal is ego satisfaction through climbing the corporate ladder rather than improving product, service, and profits. For them, solving system problems takes too much sharing of ideas, resources, risks, and credit. Professional career managers' promotions should be based on team participation, and nothing else. (If this doesn't work, let them go outside and dust the erasers or something.)

The presence of system problems means that a total and lasting solution is not local: upper management must correct system problems, either directly or through totally empowered interdepartmental teams. This requires individuals to "own up" to their responsibility for the problems. This is why "insiders" often have difficulty pushing the Deming philosophy throughout the company.

In short, how do you know you have system problems? You

can normally "feel it." System problems are interdepartmental and/or beyond control of the frontline employees. I have normally found six to eight issues like the following add up nonlinearly to cause the system problem—no single one could account for the predicament:

• There are ineffective employee selection procedures. The company needs to quiz recruits on current events to see if they are eggheads. If they cannot tell you about the Deming philosophy, let the competition have them. They must be permanently anesthetized if they do not know about the roulette wheel by now.
• Wages are below community average and only the uninspired hang around.
• Creative employees are stymied by the number crunchers.
• There are no useful raw material specifications.
• The sales force is not knowledgeable of process capabilities.
• Purchasing employees are not aware of operational needs.
• There are outdated job descriptions.
• There is poor or insufficient training for both new-hires and long-timers.
• There is a lack of preventative maintenance (mechanics like to "fix," not to prevent).
• Competing objectives are imposed by management.
• Vendor shopping for lowest purchase price occurs. There is little concern for quality.
• The accounting system rewards only short-term results.
• There is an unawareness of internal customer needs.
• Political clout is needed to get maintenance performed.

And the list goes on as you look into the deep, dark abyss of failure.

As it applies to managing a business, you have just grasped the equivalent of a master's degree in statistics. When reading the upcoming chapters you will learn how to use this knowledge. The best intuition for a manager to have is numerical intuition—the vision of the uncertainty of the numerical outcome of the roulette wheel and the bell curve on the table. I heard an industry sage say, "Don't do something, just stand there!" Let this stuff incubate. Take a five-minute mental break and reflect on how the roulette wheel applies to system problems and business obstructions you've experienced.

This contrast between local faults and common causes is part of the all-encompassing *profound knowledge* of Deming. There's so much confusion about the other parts of his multifaceted concept of profound knowledge that I dedicated a later chapter to it.

Deming uncovered a most basic problem in common management practices: our tendency to treat system problems—the random aberrations of the roulette wheel—as controllable local faults. (Symbolically, the spin of the roulette wheel yielded a result we didn't like, but we handle the situation as if the device is off its hinges. Remember that only management can change the odds of the roulette wheel.) Then management inappropriately expects the frontline employees to just "get it done." This is a major reason *why things go wrong*. When we don't make the important distinction between common causes and local faults, not only do the employees fail to solve the difficulties in a lasting and profitable way, they burn out and form protective shells around themselves. That is because management holds them responsible for things they can't control. (The final result is worse than it first looks. People often get physically sick when held responsible for things they can't control. Someone estimated the cost of unnecessary stress-related illnesses exceeds $100 billion per year.)

A former client said once, "I had the scrap problem whipped. Then I went to Italy for six weeks, and it came right back while I was gone. What's the world coming to?" Have you ever heard this? We know now that there were system problems hidden in the bureaucracy and political quicksand. The plant manager, however, had treated the predicament as a local fault. His *bandaid* came off, or the *relief valve* erupted in his absence. He had to be right there at all times to prop up the situation. This is a typical scenario when you mistake system problems as easily fixable local faults. A unified implementation of Deming's concepts eventually gave him a lasting solution to the waste dilemma. Employees eliminated the root causes, and the boss did not have to look over shoulders to keep the progress from fading. I'll risk a generalization here: It seems that the most effective managers I meet these days are making a major effort to work themselves out of a job. Of course they do not lose their livelihood, but maybe this behavior is the key to success in this decade.

So that's the basic theory. There is no need to argue the philosophy to co-workers who don't want to hear and have not read this book. I have tried. You can't win an argument with ignorant people. It's like showing a wristwatch to a pig. It sees but does not understand. Have them read this book, let the theory incubate over a weekend and then start talking. We must imprint the concept of the roulette wheel on everyone's brain. The frontliners cannot change the odds of the roulette wheel by themselves. It will take several months for this information to sink in, so don't force people into a corner too quickly. This only motivates them to take a stand against the new philosophy. Then you have an ego battle to fight along with all your other obstacles. According to Picasso, "Every act of creation is first an act of destruction." You slowly destroy out-dated management philosophy. Consider the fifteen-year-old situation below.

A previous boss called me in to discuss a problem we had with secretarial errors. By asking the following questions I was able to conclude there were perpetual system problems and a totally empowered interdepartmental team was needed:

• Has this problem existed, more or less, at the same average level over time? *Yes*

- Has it been about the same as the faces changed? *Yes*
- Has there been variation, but did things always bounce back to the other side of average? *Yes*
- Has direct management pressure helped? *No*
- Could a group of stodgy bureaucrats—more interested in the chain of command and covering up issues to stay out of trouble—eliminate the root causes? *No*

Bingo—We had a system problem.

The process was stable (in control), but unacceptable. If we had collected data on secretarial errors, can you see how the roulette wheel and the developing bell curve would demonstrate a stable process? The interdepartmental team that we formed found eight to ten reasons for the problem, none of which the secretaries controlled. These included telephone interruptions, copying machine being in their work area and being used by managers who had not been trained to run the machine, people being uninformed of typing lead times, and the secretaries themselves being confused about standard operating procedures.

These and other system problems rendered a disruptive work environment. We implemented the team's ranked list of recommendations, and typing errors fell by 70 percent. The out-of-pocket cost was about $50. A small but significant detail of how we did this comes to mind: We conducted the inter-departmental-team brainstorming sessions in several exercises, a few days apart. This allowed time for ideas to incubate and also prevented incomplete conclusions. Don't let a conclusion be the result of an occasion where people simply get tired of thinking during a long meeting.

You always ask yourself a question when you look at a list of problems like the one above for the typing errors: Why hadn't they told us about these problems? The answer is, they probably had, but at the wrong times. They had presented immediate excuses for recent mistakes at times when our mood was neither creative nor receptive. A burning barn is an emergency and looks like a local fault. If the barn has been catching on fire a lot lately, however, it may imply system problems—ones that we'll never resolve if people work on them only as the barn blazes.

We had worn the secretaries down over the years. Their comments were typical of what I hear every week in the trenches:

> "No one ever asked me about it."
> "They'd never listen anyway."
> "I'm not paid enough to think."
> "I told the supervisor twice. What does it take?"
> "Some engineer would steal the credit."

A more obscure issue also existed. The secretaries had told us about many of the issues, but one at a time. Our response had been, "That single problem could not explain all these mistakes." We were all correct, the secretaries and management. System problems are usually numerous, and no single suggestion seems to be *the* answer. Instead, the solutions interact and add up in confusing ways. One solution would be to form an ad hoc interdepartmental (cross-functional) team. This group creates and implements a list of ranked action items. It is the combined, synergistic effect of the team approach that makes it all work. I heard an analogy to well digging in a seminar once. The struggling, lone wolf-type guy may stubbornly continue to dig a deeper hole. However, an interdepartmental team may take a broader approach and choose to "dig the hole" someplace else.

Books listed in the References and appendix A contain many good ideas on how to run interdepartmental teams. *Note:* We must teach the team participants how to form a composite, ranked list of action items. (Out-of-pocket costs impact the priority.) Then, management *must* follow their decisions, with no cherry picking. The employees' spirits won't survive many flops, regardless what they tell you. On a positive note, I have seen these teams solve forty-year-old system problems that the bureaucrats and "organizational men" had written off long ago as "the nature of the beast." All problems have solutions, but not necessarily by the bureaucracy—where employees stay entombed in a box on an organization chart. I heard a cynic say after seeing the results of one of these successful teams: "At least now they don't have any excuses for failure." I said, "I'll take that."

In the next chapter you'll learn about Dr. Deming's *fourteen points,* the *deadly diseases,* and the *obstacles*—explicit things to watch out for or to do. You just finished the longest chapter. The remaining sections each take ten minutes to read, more or less. Now skim appendix A about interdepartmental teams. You'll need at least an elemental understanding of this concept as you analyze the remaining chapters.

CHAPTER 2

The Basic Outline

Deming identified seven global problems with our ways of operating a business. He considered them so universal and devastating that he named them the *deadly diseases* of management. (I listed them in appendix B and discuss each throughout the remaining chapters.) An example is the use of formalized, written performance appraisals, whereby managers must rank employees or fit them into strata with quotas. As you'll see, many of management's "sacred cows" are actually counterproductive diseases. You can't implement the Deming philosophy unless you eliminate the firm's deadly diseases, and it may be tough. Deming said the transition isn't for the weak or timid. Nor is it for the "articulate incompetent" who can talk, but is unable to act.

Deeply rooted in the status quo, the diseases are things *not to do.* On the more positive side, Deming also provided his *fourteen points,* or things *to do.* Some of them are straightforward. Several seem obscure; they are more a way of thinking than something to write on your to-do list. As I introduce them, don't let the obscure points discourage you from implementing the clear-cut ones while you continue to learn.

You may have already implemented some of the fourteen points as a result of common sense, but probably not to the extent that Deming recommended. The other points may seem foreign to you. In the course of more than a hundred hands-on consulting clients, I have found it necessary to implement *all* fourteen points—in some cases to finish what someone else had started, but in most situations to begin from ground zero. It will be worth your effort. Because of the routine bureaucratic issues on their desks begging for attention, managers pass *eighty* percent of their time on the *twenty* percent of the topics that yield the least profit. This is an example of the **Pareto Principle,** the **80-20 rule.** How many times have you almost missed a deadline on an extremely important project because "must-do," trifling matters distracted you? (If you don't manage your life, someone else will.) When managers internalize the Deming philosophy, everything they do revolves around one of the fourteen points—the major issues. As a result, some of the trivia eventually goes away.

Each chapter in this book pertains to one of the fourteen points. The arrangement is more or less in the order I would begin the implementation. The points overlap, both among themselves and with the diseases. I don't know why Deming did this—perhaps for emphasis. Don't let the seeming redundancy confuse you.

I have also included a chapter about barriers so typical Deming named them **obstacles.** It helps to know about your problems in advance. Smart people learn from their own mistakes, while brilliant people learn from others' blunders. Plan a strategy to deal with the obstacles before they arise.

Now to the first point, ranking performance appraisals, which is also a disease—and the most hallowed of sacred cows. Many creative acts require that something be destroyed. Sacred cows make great steaks. It's slaughter time.

CHAPTER 3

Return Pride of Workmanship

The acid that often curdles working relationships is pride coupled with the belief that one's ability and creativity aren't being used. If we instill in the workplace a small fraction of the self-satisfaction the employees take in their hobbies and civic activities, the bottom line will flourish. As Deming said, the typical firm's bottom line profit could be twice its present level. I didn't believe this when I heard it in 1980, but I've seen it happen. From increased frontline excitement, a twenty-five percent improvement is common with a complete Deming transition, the extent of which you may not be able to grasp until you have completed this book. Different firms have unique deficiencies, but there is a common thread—enthusiasm is inadequate almost everywhere. And I do not mean eagerness to impress the boss. We have a great deal of that. What is inadequate is excitement toward improving the product, process, service, or productivity—whether or not an "attaboy" is expected. We can't expect greater devotion merely by asking for it, however. We have to remove demotivators.

Thoroughly implementing the Deming tools will help achieve a higher level of stimulation in the organization. Logic and creativity—for a change—outpace politics and personal agendas. The newfound objectivity invites suppressed talent to the surface and helps match reality and expectations. Philosophically, co-workers evaluate each other by their above-board actions. But we judge ourselves mostly by our capabilities. It is wonderful when the Deming transition helps equate the capabilities and the demonstrated actions.

For salaried employees, one of the worst morale busters is the written performance appraisal system that requires rankings, some quota of 1s, 2s, 3s, 4s, and 5s, or some other disguised ordering. Deming lists ranking performance appraisals as a disease and as part of one of his fourteen points. *Note:* I recommend more *qualitative,* structured feedback—assuming there is no rater bias and the evaluator is not the stoic, demotivating type. The numbers, those rankings and quotas, are the vampires that suck the pride of workmanship and teamwork motivations from the employees.

It is as simple as this: Ranking employees against their peers during the performance appraisal process may excite a trifling few who win, but this gain is a drop in the bucket compared to the oceans-full of morale lost among the many. To quote Norman Cousins, "Death is not the greatest loss in life. The greatest loss is what dies in us while we live."

Most firms have no ranking performance appraisal, so those of you in the remaining companies that do will have to sharpen your scalpels to be ready to perform frontal-lobe lobodomies on the diehards who still insist on them. There can be no compromising here if you want to be a Deming company.

Do not discount the need here. Many top managers deservedly rose on a fast track during their climb to the summit. They understandably don't comprehend the damage done to a *solid citizen* when the boss says during a performance appraisal, *"You are below average."* Especially when the system and things beyond employees' control are often largely to blame. (Remember the roulette wheel and bell curve again.) For *any* group, even the astronauts or the Rockettes, half are below average. Why tell them? This elicits too many unexpected reactions. It is easy to underestimate the damage done by these appraisals, because people seldom complain verbally. They usually know that superiors expect them to be tough enough to take such frank talk. They do, however, often take covert action. Research shows that a whopping one-third of the salaried employees in this country have their resumes out. You obviously don't hear about it. Behind the scenes, however, they normally "pull down the hatches." As a result, the workplace becomes an every-man-for-himself environment. When people form these protective shells around themselves, *things go wrong*. Many technical problems don't get solved.

Psychologists find that we usually treat successes as our own but blame failure on the system, or others. Workers tune out if we tell them they are failing when the system is to blame. They respond by daydreaming for psychological survival. (They appear absentminded, but may be presentminded someplace else.) But they tune in when you show them they are successful. As a consultant, I often shiver at the improvement opportunities that are "oozing out of the woodwork" when I visit some clients. I usually find that the employees have tuned out and fallen into ruts. Over time the shouting opportunities became whispers—and then were gone.

In any firm the employees' perceived performances mostly follow the roulette wheel and bell curve. If the process is in control, a great deal of the variation you see among the employees is from uncontrollable system aberrations—ones mostly beyond the workers' domination. This is part of Deming's profound knowledge, and a component that I have always found to be true. Once again, visualize the bell on the tabletop. An employee perceived as exactly average is at the bull's-eye. One acknowledged as a nonperformer falls off the left of the table onto the floor. Most of the rest of bell personifies the solid citizens—the people who do most of the work, but whom we've demoralized and frustrated the most. For these people collectively, system common cause variability far exceeds any actual differences in their abilities or efforts. Ranking or categorizing them with quotas causes weird psychological reactions. Granted, there are two to five percent who are truly horrible, or terrific. It is easy to identify these extreme cases (called outliers by statisticians)—they are undeniably different because of God-given talent and energy, or lack of it. You do not have to rank everyone to identify these extreme cases. For the solid citizens representing ninety-five to ninety-eight percent of the remaining population, it is especially harmful to use ranking systems to dole out routine raises or praises. (Of course, immediate and undocumented "attaboys" or frowns for specific acts are still advised when everyone knows the expectations.)

Many managers see the written performance appraisal system as bureaucratic overmanagement and a waste of time. They will actually cheer when you abolish it. However, when you stop ranking, you still have to deal with the small number of employees in the bell-curve extremes—at the very edges of the table. The one to two percent on the high (right) side of the bell are obviously superior. Treat them accordingly.

You must relocate the small percentage in the low end of the bell to another job—perhaps to a competitor. There's an outside chance that drastically different training may help, but something must be done. When you return pride of workmanship to the company, the solid citizens will request that this two to three percent either carry their weight or get relocated.

I have asked hundreds of times and learned that few managers up the hierarchy ever look at the written performance appraisals anyway. You base the big personnel decisions on gut feeling. Don't let anyone persuade you to punish the masses by following his advice to use numerical rankings to fire a few people legally, or to boost several other people's egos. Other ways exist. Rid yourself of this disease in one fell swoop—there is no room for compromise.

Deming said that management's greatest dread is dealing with people problems. Ranking performance appraisals do not get this people issue off your desk.

In summary:
- Do employees still need timely feedback? *Yes*
- Do you need to train and prod most managers to get them to provide feedback? *Yes*
- Do you need or want a formal performance appraisal system that ranks people? *No*
- Do people need career guidance from elders? *Yes*

During the official performance appraisal process, let the workers have some pride. In response, they may show more interest in the total goals of the firm, rather than having to watch the boss on a continuing basis to make sure they get a good written performance appraisal. This **boss watching** is a major cancer spoiling many firms' profitability. How can we expect teamwork when unnecessary internal competition and excessive catering to the boss's whims abound? Enlightened leaders deserve, and generally want, objective and creative advice. Let's direct our ruinous efforts toward the outside competitors and the cruel marketplace, not each other. (Do you see why some power-hungry managers and company politicians hate Deming? Level with and defuse them upfront.)

Boss watching also destroys creativity. The "voice of judgment," whether from within your own psyche or from the boss, and our constant struggle to impress others obliterates creativity. Most humans are innately survivalists. Our brains first deal with the most immediate issue—at times even when we are not aware of it. The "big, bad wolf at the door" is often the boss, so we all want to live in the "brick house that he cannot blow down." Things can be different. Have you ever noticed how you get some brilliant, creative ideas when on vacation where things have time to incubate? Expect *things to go wrong* when people do not have an opportunity to be creative on the job because of fear and the constant struggle to impress others. We need innovations. In five years you will be doing nothing the way you do it today. Think back five years and you will see the truth of this.

There are additional ways to return pride of workmanship to the salaried employees, but eliminating the performance appraisal rankings is the only one that fits this
Deming point. Implementing the total Deming transition
will also help return enthusiasm because management based
on facts will replace motivations from politics and fear. I'll
never forget the words of an old minister: "They that worship
God merely from fear would worship the devil too, if he
appear." People want to be able to have pride in their motivations.

Deming had a great deal more to say about returning pride
of workmanship to the remaining employees—the hourly and
nonmanagement frontline workers. Many of them trade time
at work for dollars, and they hate it. They want to do more.
They know enough not to complain repeatedly, and what they
do tell their superiors often gets filtered and misinterpreted.
Therefore, you may not always know exactly how these workers feel. Here's a sample of what I heard from them just
within the last month:

The boss makes us ship bad quality.
We don't trust Bill. He lied to us.
Joe's a people-hating S.O.B. as a supervisor, but management
    won't remove him.
They cut our pay by 10 percent, but management got a raise.
I could show them 20 inexpensive improvements that would
    improve profits by 15 percent in a matter of weeks, but no
    one has asked or would listen. Now, some 23-year-old engi-
    neer installed a $300,000 *gadget* that actually hurt the
    process.
Our foreman won the "man of the year" award when we know
    he is a jerk who steals everybody's credit.
We used to be able to flag down a maintenance person to get
    the machine worked on. Now we have to track down the
    foreman, who tells the "new" maintenance coordinator,
    who then decides if and when someone accomplishes our
    repairs. How can we run this job? Another layer of

management now exists to slow the work. It takes days sometimes to get something fixed. (An occasional mistake, we
can afford—bureaucratic overmanagement, we cannot.)

We are all receptive now to the idea of employee empowerment and the venting of discontent, but frustrations still
exist among the frontline workers. In management's defense,
however, about half of the problem is poor communications
(both ways).

Here is what Deming had to say about returning pride of
workmanship to frontline jobs:

Never turn down any moderate request for funds or action if
it can be demonstrated there is a sure improvement in
pride of workmanship. The unforeseen, psychological
return on investment will amaze all doubters.

Establish realistic quality assurance standards (specs) and
never ship nonconforming product. I have seen many cases
where management intentionally made the specs too strin-
gent to keep the workers on their toes. However, in an
emergency, the foreman could overrule the inspector.
Employees are far too smart to accept this outdated practice any longer.

Redefine the job of most engineers and many managers.
Instead of saying, "It is your job to find and implement
improvements," stand up to them with the following direc-
tive: "It is your job to develop and implement the recomen-
dations of the frontline employees." If you can accomplish
this, be ready to explain to your superiors why you never
achieved this high level of profitability before. (If
someone would only say this to young engineers and MBAs
just out of college!)

Teach the employees about the ***extended process.*** If they know
how the suppliers' actions affect their jobs, and how their
own variability impacts the guy down the line, their jobs
become more fulfilling. Their decisions will be more

accurate. Pay to have them visit vendors and customers. The returns will be impressive.

Get an independent outsider with a "down-home" bedside manner to "wade around in the rice patties" to elicit recommendations from the frontline workers. What gets uncovered will amaze you.

Allocate ten percent of your maintenance or capital improvement budget to the frontline workers, to spend and prioritize as they see fit. When they realize "This is really going to happen," they become realistic. The expensive, off-the-wall requests generally subside.

Get upper management to talk routinely to the frontline workers.

Most of you could add a dozen items to the list above to enhance pride of workmanship. The bottom line: When the employees care, there is enthusiasm; and when we listen to them and follow through, profits come. This is especially true of service employees. Nothing will help bad service issues if management continually frustrates the frontline workers— the ones who come in contact with the customers. Managers have to bend over backwards to keep these people in a cheery mood. It's that simple. It has been suggested that one dissatisfied customer has the ability to turn away 250 potential buyers. The bureaucracy cannot "manage" itself to better service.

Some words are the ties that bind civilization together over the centuries: "There is nothing better for a man than to rejoice in his work" (Ecclesiastes 3:22). The root word for enthusiasm is the Greek *enthousiasmos,* which means "the God within you." Take away this "birthright" and you can expect *things to go wrong.* You may never know the true philosophical reason from complaints. Conquering-hero Hollywood scripts and our hard-bitten ancestors conditioned us to be pragmatic and nonphilosophical at work—you know, the strong, silent type. This attitude was appropriate in pioneer days, but not now in large organizations.

CHAPTER 4

Take All Steps
to Drive Out Fear

Fear. Our most powerful management tool of yesteryear no longer makes money for the company. It can only achieve a minimal level of half-hearted, short-term effort while the employees are looking for other jobs—either actively, or psychologically while on company time. B. F. Skinner said so accurately, "The person who has been chastised, at best, learns how to avoid punishment." There is little creativity. The subconscious mind takes the path of least resistance to survive. If it were not that way, our species would have become extinct.

Theoretically, extreme anxiety may help some people appropriately respond to emergencies (the roulette wheel off its hinges), but it is unfitting for the more typical, perennial system problems. Management must help outline in advance what constitutes an emergency so that anxiety, when needed, can be mostly self-imposed. Then the boss does not have to risk eliciting unexpected responses, for which the workers begrudge later.

We kindly and incorrectly attribute most fear to the system, but practically all employee apprehension comes from managers and their actions. Even those trying to follow Deming have often not removed all the fear; and on occasion that has been intentional. Let me clarify one concern to loosen the resistance: Eliminating fear is not the same as turning your head from faulty work or despicable practices. Employees must have an *awareness of the consequences* of intolerable actions. Fear results from uncertainty and a feeling of no control; that's different from a healthy awareness of the consequences. Knowledge of the repercussions may not make people ecstatic, but it does not give them that sick feeling in their stomachs as they dress for work in the morning in the way that fear does. *Things go wrong* because of fear, not because people are aware of reasonable consequences.

You can take hundreds of actions to attempt to motivate the employees and to increase profits, but few of them will have a predictable impact when employees harbor fear. If anxiety prevails, you usually don't hear about it because fright prevents them from telling you. As a consultant, I have had hundreds of opportunities to investigate why good programs and procedures fizzled over the years. In almost all cases, fear prowled in the background. The workers had learned through trial and error how to avoid punishment. And that's all. In the presence of fear, you can't inspire them to take risks or to be more creative.

Some of the consequences of fear that lead to high costs, poor quality, accidents, and lost customers:

- Burnout
- Stress-related diseases
- Mediocrity
- Departmentalization and high costs ("That's not my job." Have you ever heard this?)
- Slanted glances at the boss when employees speak during meetings
- Lots of unpredictable reactions to management's attempts to improve profitability
- No initiative; waiting for orders
- Most common concern: "What will (name of boss) think about this?"

A small number of chiefs will never strive to reduce the fear in their departments. Neutralize them now. If you don't, you may be out too, after a buyout, downsizing, or a reorganization. (This isn't an attempt to instill fear, simply an *awareness of the consequences*.) As part of improving performance, the manager's job is to minimize the "net organizational pain." Sometimes ridding the firm of one "people-punisher" eliminates a thousand times as much anguish across the rest of the work force. Removing a tumor often saves the rest of the body. We have generally associated the concept of lifetime employment with Deming, but he never said you should not remove the people-punishers. He did say, however, that the number one goal of all managers must be lifetime security of the masses through good management practices—not mere verbal guarantees to cover bad management practices.

A theory of mine explains why fear accumulates over time: the skeletons often stay in the closet, and build up, after the source disappears. This is the ***dead-boss theory***. Employees never forget. It usually takes more continued energy to remove the skeletons than it did to put them there. The bones become dislodged and are difficult to clean up. Time heals the wounds too slowly—if at all. We are creatures of habit. Fear avoidance becomes implanted.

For example, I once discovered that a purchasing clerk made three copies of each transaction for different file cabinets in separate rooms, when she only needed one imprint. The copying and filing took her about five hours per week. She explained that ten years ago a previous boss almost fired her when a new employee destroyed an entire drawer, and a document the supervisor later needed was unavailable. My comment: "But he's gone." Her response: a deep-socket stare. I was looking into a dark abyss of fear, and it was looking back at me. Are two extra copies by this worker a big deal? Yes. Multiply this by several thousand to cover the entire company, and it's a big, big deal. Someone needed to say, "You don't have to do that anymore."

The dead-boss theory applies almost everywhere. Find the skeletons in the closet. (Academicians have reviewed this book to make sure that I paid homage to those before me.

Note: The dead-boss theory is closely related to Maslow's hierarchy of needs theory.)

About fifty percent of the time, when I investigated, the employees could not support the fear they felt with recent facts, but that does not matter. Their anxiety still warranted management action. Even if the fear is from monstrous actions of the past—gone and buried with some jerk supervisor—it still takes as much overt action by the present managers to remove the skeletons from the closet as it took the previous bad guys to put them there. Fear from misconceptions and communication problems won't go away on its own, at least not for ten to fifteen years. Implementing the other parts of the Deming philosophy will help reduce the level of future fear as you base decisions less on politics and personal agendas, but that alone won't be enough to eliminate the skeletons in the closet. Consider the explicit steps below and create a more detailed list of your own. This is a long list—it takes a concentrated effort to remove fear. Time may heal some wounds, but way too slowly for a profit-seeking company.

• Create a committee that does the firing so we discharge no one unfairly as a knee jerk.

• Write clearer job descriptions and requirements with scheduled reviews and updates. (What am I supposed to be doing?)

• Set up more specific specifications. (Will I get into trouble if we ship this?)

• Institute severance pay for those discontinued. (This is so that those left behind don't envision deprived families in soup-kitchen lines.)

• Do exit interviews a year after people leave the firm. Now, secure in their new jobs, they may tell you about the "troll in the three-piece suit."

• Announce to all managers that you will *not* tolerate the use of fear. (Remember the *awareness-of-consequences* discussion?)

• Implement evaluations revolving around: "What are you doing to eliminate fear?"

• Quickly eliminate of one or two people-punishers from direct supervision; tell the others why; and then announce, "Relax, the house is clean." Don't forget the dead-boss theory, however. You'll still have to remove the skeletons from the closet.

• Pay a few misfits to go away. Don't wait for their next honest mistake to fire them. If you do, the question of the year becomes, "Who's next? I wonder what level of mistake I'd have to make to get canned?" How can the remaining employees be creative in that kind of atmosphere?

• Consider that we put ninety percent of the nonperformers in the wrong job, or they received inadequate training. (A later point in this book addresses the fallacy of on-the-job training [OJT] as the sole training method.) Employees who repeatedly have problems because of a need of training will not likely benefit from more of the same type of instruction. They need something different. Another dose of the same medicine will not help.

• Analyze your office mannerisms. Employees overreact to the subliminal messages, such as:

The fear of being "called into the boss's office." Visit them on their turf.
Friday afternoon reprimands and firings, and the ruined weekends.
Being greeted at 8:05 A.M. with a stern face: "Sam, can you come into my office at 4 P.M. today? We've got to talk." See him right now, or else call him nearer to the designated time.
If this attitude is seemingly implied: "Your time is not important. I can be late for meetings. I'm the boss."
If this attitude is seemingly implied: "I am so more important than you that it's okay for you to sit outside my office and wait on me to call you in at my convenience."

"I want to know who's to blame for this! I'll have his butt." If you motivate employees to take the attitude of defending mistakes, there will be no hope of improvement. It isn't good to pin every mistake on somebody. Eighty to ninety percent of your unfavorable occurrences come from a complex and interacting chain of common cause (system) events.

I worked with an innovative manager once who totally changed his intended management style, from fear-inducing to nurturing. Nevertheless, not much improved. His continued mannerisms, like the ones above, unintentionally sent the same old message of fear.

The only constructive fear comes from the innovations of your external competitors and the unpredictability of the marketplace. The employees will respect this on their own if they know the facts. Don't threaten them. Fear elicits too many unexpected responses. Like some managers, employees often kill messengers. Figure out a way to let them learn the discouraging news of the marketplace without you having to personally threaten them.

The other parts of the Deming transition will help reduce fear, especially internalization of the concept of the roulette wheel. Variability is a fact of life, and we cannot hold people responsible for every aberration away from the norm. There's no excuse for some of the stress people have to tolerate. The roulette wheel applies to weekly sales, service times, resource usage, and so forth. Expecting every week to be better than average not only defies the statistical laws of nature, but dooms the frontliners of burnout, subsequent failure, and fear. This explains *why things go wrong*. The net result is lower long-term profits and lots of smoke screens. Continued long-term improvement is more important than ever; but as you will read later, we now have to approach improvement differently.

I often hear: "We've reached a plateau and can't get any better. The two most frequent root causes I uncover are fear and hidden management by the numbers. The results: There is no energy left to creatively improve the processes. There is no time to escape the rat race. There is no time to learn what to do with the time if we had it. Hence, we end up in stagnation. The relief valves cause things to go wrong and you often do not know why. Managers cover up their problems. A typical relief valve is wasted effort having to "manage those above us," which leaves little time to nurture those below. I refer to this as *reverse management.*

CHAPTER 5

Eliminate All Banners and Slogans Asking for New Levels of Effort

Not a gigantic issue, but take down all banners and posters asking people to work harder. Achieving better work doesn't come about from a technique as simple as tacking up a banner. The employees need road maps, not clichés. A few ridiculous examples of banner exhortations:

- Safety Is Your Responsibility (Who wants to get hurt?)
- Work Smart, Not Hard (Who wants to sweat and suffer?)
- Quality Comes First (Only actions prove this.)

I know we can get a "warm, fuzzy" feeling after doing *something*. Putting up banners is at least *something*. But the employees laugh at them under their breath. In the name of Deming, take them down. This is a good first place to start, and do it before the masses read this book.

One possible exception: Is it okay to have a bulletin board with a few entertaining and motivational flyers? Maybe so, if you change them weekly and don't, in any way, imply that management sees this as "getting the people issue off their desks." A hilarious cartoon on a bulletin board may be OK. A chuckle can foster creativity. These banners may be OK also:

Women
Men
Open Hole
Danger
Bad Dog

CHAPTER 6

Move in the Direction of Sole Sourcing for All Goods and Services—Stop Buying Based on Price Tag Alone

Many firms are already using single suppliers for purchased goods and services. They seldom blindly buy from the lowest bidder anymore. Switching from vendor to vendor in manufacturing generally costs you five times what you seem to save in low purchase prices. The workers can tell you that. The same is true in the service sector, although the jury rigs are not as visible there. Service workers, at a cost, can usually compensate for many of the problems caused by switching vendors. You don't hear about many of these profit-draining jury rigs. (Workers stand as tough and persistent in this country as John Paul Jones.)

Why move in the direction of sole sourcing? There are many reasons. As Deming taught, to minimize waste and to be competitive, we must consider the extended process—not only our own operations, but relations with suppliers and users. Adversarial relationships and arms-length dealings among suppliers and users reduce everyone's profits (except the lawyers). These short-term, low-bidder relationships require that no firm commit to another or tool-up for the long haul. How can vendors commit to research and cost-cutting investments if they can only sell in the spot market? Elusive things go wrong when this situation occurs.

The following types of obvious administrative costs are also excessive with multiple sourcing:

• Travel costs to many vendor locations
• Increased paperwork and long distance calls
• Excessive inventory carrying costs to compensate for bad quality
• Inability to reap quantity discounts
• Spreading of confidential information

After a firm makes the transition to sole sourcing, an outsider often has difficulty telling who works for the vendor and which employees represent the buying firm. Do purchase prices go up when you sole source? *No.* Over hundreds of cases, I have only seen acquisition costs go down, as profits went up for everyone. We call the new relationship among sellers and buyers a *partnership.*

Start training the purchasing employees first, and now. They will be the most threatened when they learn there will be no more "attaboys" for low prices, unless they can also prove the total associated costs across the entire company are minimal. Lots of good books, consultants, and seminars exist on vendor certification and partnershipping. (Contact the American Society for Quality Control, 1-800-248-1946.)

Vendor quality is in the hearts of their employees, not in a bureaucratic manual or flow chart. National quality awards or formal supplier systems can deceive you. For example, ISO 9000 (the documented quality standard created by the European Economic Community) may be important, but certification does not really mean a vendor's quality and service are the best in the industry. It only denotes that the vendor incurred the expense of documenting a certain "acceptable" level of quality. (Of course, that is of some interest and could break a tie among vendor-hopefuls.)

Announce in public that the direction toward sole sourcing is not optional. State that in one to two years the firm will be working with considerably fewer vendors. But be patient. It takes about three years to form and nurture a true vendor partnership: one where each party helps solve the other's problems because their survival depends on mutual cooperation.

In most cases, it only makes sense to let the frontline workers decide who the supplier will be. Many firms form three or four-person ad hoc interdisciplinary teams to select vendors. Let this group establish what smaller number of vendors they will have and the acceptance criteria.

If you don't trust a chosen vendor, you have not done your homework. If you find you got rooked by a supplier, it is because you didn't do your background investigations well enough in the beginning. What are the chances that you would *not* be well advised to sole source—or at least reducing from seven or eight to two or three suppliers? The probability is about equal to that of going on a picnic and getting caught in a hailstorm. It's not impossible, but it is unlikely.

Another of Deming's deadly diseases is the *excessively short-term orientation of managers*. This disease fits well with the point of this chapter. Penny pinchers—who know the cost of everything but the value of nothing—find it too tempting to do anything but take the short-term approach to purchasing. They will only look at the up-front price of purchased items until management directs otherwise. It is easy to defend themselves by pointing out, "But I bought at the lowest price!"

Simply providing specifications and slapping wrists when suppliers don't conform to them yields mediocre quality and service. *When you buy the product, you also buy the process that will make the future output.* Don't be afraid to audit vendors and to make them read this book. First, and foremost, make sure they don't possess the deadly diseases. This especially applies to the one described in the next chapter: managing the business mostly by the numbers. If they still participate in this archaic practice, you can bet their product and service contain many hidden defects and unnecessary costs. Go elsewhere. (I may have just saved you millions of dollars and zillions of headaches!)

CHAPTER 7

Eliminate Management by the Numbers

"If you can measure it, you can control it" isn't true. It never was, regardless what we learned from the old textbooks. The falsity of that outdated motto is at the heart of Deming's philosophy. The numbers, at times, can tell you if you previously met expectations. That is about all. Using hoped-for financial wishes as pie-in-the-sky objectives to express desires or threats (from the front office) leads to unpredictable and usually unimpressive results. I heard an office manager jokingly compare this practice to an out-of-touch miser who wants his family to use less electricity. He sits outside his home all day with his eye on the electric meter. When it moves too fast, he pounds on the window and shakes his finger at his wife and kids.

Anyone can bang on the window. The tightwad needs a plan for improving. A more capable home economist would rarely look at the meter, but instead would go inside the house to elicit energy-saving suggestions and commitment from the family members. Can you see the analogy with running a business?

Financial reports contain important facts, and we often need better accountability for the numbers. But improving performance and quality is never quite as simple as threatening with numerical wishes. Innovative managers today don't intimidate with numbers, nor do they state objectives in pass-fail quantitative terms. These approaches only get you to about a 1970s level of competitiveness. Good managers stay close to the process and expect their subordinates to provide a constant stream of process-improving plans. We call this "moving away from the quantitative to the qualitative." Inspiring leaders respond to the frontline workers' suggestions and in turn expect measurable improvements on a continuing basis. The key words are *improvements on a continuing basis.* They have no numerical goal you either make, or don't make. For example, if the average scrap rate is presently 6 percent, and you receive—from above—a goal of 5 percent, don't you deserve praise if you get it down to a sustainable 5.3 percent?

Heavy reliance on numerical results as a major management tool is both a Deming disease and one of his points. I could provide 800 pages of examples I know of where managing by the numbers has reduced profits by the millions, but to keep this book short, I will provide it in far fewer pages. (I promised to keep this book short.)

Before explaining why management by the numbers is one of the deadly diseases, let me say that we'll always have financial summaries and a bottom line. These are our report cards. Long-term prosperity comes from repeated periods of short-term success. But it is risky to give people short-term numerical objectives. The roulette wheel makes it difficult to even know what sustained numbers are possible. On the other hand, near-term qualitative goals and plans are a must.

We occasionally have to put up pennies of effort now to reap dollars later. Deming gave a warning for analyzing moderate improvement ideas: Never use business-school financial calculations (like net-present-value) to turn down modest requests for funding when it is obvious the expenditure would enhance quality, service, and pride of workmanship. The unknowns and unknowables are five to ten times more important to profits than the things you can readily count. An example of the unknowns and unknowables: Can you quantify the income flow from improved pride of workmanship and the resulting search by the employees for ways to improve the product and processes? Use quantitative capital expenditure methods only for huge expenditures requiring outside financing.

I have never seen a single case where thoughtfully eradicating the by-the-numbers disease, even for a moment, caused us to have to sacrifice short-term finances for the long term. For some people, this statement defies logic, but trust me. I have been in the middle of it many times.

Managing by the numbers today is taboo in most circles, even for those who do not know of Dr. Deming's teachings. I suppose that is why most executives, when confronted by me, give me a deep-socket stare when they say, "I do not manage by numerical quotas anymore!" I believe them, but always find islands of by-the-numbers management in their companies. It takes long-term, extensive effort by the top guys to eradicate this disease. When middle management has been rewarded for years for meeting a numerical quota, they are not likely to let go just because the big boss says once or twice, "We are not going to manage by the numbers anymore."

A further clarifying remark before I convince you of the calamity of by-the-numbers management: In a desperate situation, it is acceptable to state the hard, quantifiable facts. If a ten percent increase in sales is the only thing that will keep you in business this year, tell that to the employees. However, you must show them the stats as to why this is true and talk more about your plans for improving, rather than asserting pie-in-the-sky numerical wishes. When you lay out the dire quantitative facts, state at the outset that this emergency mode is temporary. When the crisis is officially over, tell the employees so that they can get into a more creative long-term spirit. Don't leave them hanging. *Warning:* I am, however, making the assumption you solved the root-cause problems, and that lack of hustle was not the original culprit. I have never seen a solitary case where lack of intensity was the cause, rather than a symptom. All people aren't inherently lazy; they want their work lives to be as satisfying as possible. Goofing off (lack of intensity) as a universal issue is a system problem: one that rests with management at some level. Maybe it is at the top—we manage the way we are managed. Our subconscious desire to fit in leads us to this.

Major problems require forceful plans, not threats. (For chronic predicaments, create totally empowered interdepartmental teams and monitor their progress.) Wishful thinking alone accomplishes very little. To quote Washington Irving, "Great minds have purposes and plans, others have wishes."

Using numerical targets or quotas to motivate people in the absence of grave situations is a fatally flawed strategy. At best, you get only the isolated (suboptimizing) number you ask for, and rarely that. If the threat is great enough, people can accomplish almost anything for a while, but you'll always suffer a trade-off in the form of a *relief valve*. Always. These relief valves cause things to go wrong in a confusing, delayed manner. Examples of profit-draining relief valves include:

• Demoralizing fatigue
• Unmeasured quality suffering
• Loss of enthusiasm and creativity
• Excessive wear on equipment (no preventive maintenance)
• *Number fudging and outright cheating (It has been estimated that half of the work done in the world is to make things appear what they aren't.)
• Loss of customers
• Worker turnover
• No creativity or synergy
• Vacillating between problems-of-the-week: quality, then quantity
• Union drive started (Almost always a relief valve)
• Accidents (A most typical relief valve when the pressure is "on.")

I added the asterisk (*) for emphasis. Sometimes the cover-up is perceived as "necessary to survive," such as depreciating an outlay that should be expensed—to look good this year—knowing that the company loses profit because of your "sharp pencil." A less despicable practice is creating five identical $1,000-dollar purchase orders for a single $5,000-item because your approval limit is too low. What's gained here? You get around the bureaucracy or upper management that does not understand your requirements. What's the net loss to the company? Time wasted on this *paper entrepreneurship,* that could be spent creating value.

As another glaring example of the evils of managing by the numbers, consider the airlines. The flyer with one of the best on-time gate pull-back percentages has among the worst total customer satisfaction records. The FAA publishes on-time pull-back percentages, not total customer satisfaction. I fly every day and do not mind taking off three minutes late. (There's a roulette wheel here that some airline managers need to consider.) I become appalled, however, when they deceitfully "lock us in" and we sit on the pad away from the gate for ninety minutes waiting for a fuel truck—especially when all the competitors' planes take off and I know I'm going to miss my next connection.

Here is another outrageous example of foolish managing by the numbers: I met a hospital admissions administrator, just last month, who has a monthly quota for the number of sick people she must admit. When she is below quota, the brass tells her she is not meeting expectations. What is she supposed to do? Hire hit men to mangle would-be customers? Or maybe release dioxin or typhoid serum into the water supply? That would bring in some sick folks.

Management by numerical objectives (MBO) and quotas achieve mediocrity, at best. If anything, you tend to elicit (for a while) only a little more of what you have been getting from the troops. To stay competitive, most firms need new recipes from the chefs—not just bigger servings of the same old stuff. If there is a complete void of motivation, managing by the numbers may quickly get you to a minimal level of profitability. You never, however, become competitive or advance beyond an early plateau. This plateau was okay in 1965, but not now. I have worked with some extreme cases as a consultant over the last twenty years. In every case where things were really bad, I always have found that numerical quotas lurked somewhere, often unofficially. These quotas were the problem, although the relief valves often disguised it.

Consider the roulette wheel and bell curve for a delivery service, and pieces of mail sorted. Assume it has an average (bull's-eye) of 13,000 pieces of mail sorted and the right and left extremes (table edges) are 16,000 and 10,000. About half the time the numbers will be unpredictably above average, and on the rest of the occasions they'll be below the norm. (This is guaranteed by the statistical laws of chance.) It is probably safe to assume the process is in control because alert employees keep the local faults at a minimum. It is the random fluctuations, the roulette wheel, they can't tame. (Stable processes are the norm. The plus-or-minus, random spread of the bell is usually surprisingly wide.)

Situations can be stable, but that does not mean they are necessarily acceptable. In the case above, let's say 13,000 is not a favorable average. How could you improve it? We've seen what will not work over the long haul: simply pushing the workers with quotas, using slogans, or creating fear. The irrefutable truth:

> You can't improve a stable system by wishful thinking or threats to attain a higher quota. The only lasting improvements can come from management. The front-line workers have good ideas, but not the resources or authority to accomplish lasting improvements. The system problems usually hide in the status quo—in the white spaces of the organization chart—and require interdisciplinary, interdepartmental teams.

This is a tough pill to take. And at first glance, this assessment often does not seem correct. However, upon detailed, objective analysis I have never been able to disprove the generalization. This undeniable, fundamental principle rests at the heart of the Deming philosophy. If you can't accept it, don't try to implement the Deming theory. You will fail. However, if you do decide to proceed with Deming's ideas, you and all of upper management must be forceful with the diehards and root out unofficial, hidden islands of by-the-numbers management.

If you must utilize numerical quotas, what goal would you use with these mail sorters? The average, thus accepting the status quo? No. In this real-life example, the actual, senseless quota management chose was 15,000. (This was 2,000 above the current natural average.) One day in a hundred, the sorters randomly hit this figure when all the system common causes added up in their favor. Most days they failed miserably and felt miserable as a result. Granted, the frontline workers know that on some days they can temporarily jury rig their way into beating the odds of the roulette wheel. Deming calls these jury rigs the infamous *knee jerks.* The mail sorters could just throw envelopes with illegible addresses into a pail. They could accelerate the machines to the point they may jam. They could skip breaks and lunch. This could go on and on ad nauseam. Using these knee jerks may meet a day's quota, but their eventual effect would yield a lowered net production for the month. A clerk announced in a team meeting once, "I don't want to learn the tricks of the trade. I want to learn the trade." I think you see the point: knee jerks waste money. (They make people look busy though, especially when it comes to fixing the resulting predicament later.) In the case of the mail sorters, as elsewhere, there was no smart numerical quota that could be used. However, in the long term, dozens of system problems existed. If management had solved them, production would be higher today.

In another example, an unseasoned, numbers-oriented hospital administrator decided that every cost center had to carry its own weight with a profit-and-loss statement. He therefore discontinued the hospital's child daycare facility. I'm sure he was quick to report his on-paper savings to his corporate superiors. (Look, Ma—No cavities!) What happened? Nurses quit in droves. They had come to depend on this service. So his largest problem, recruiting nurses, elevated to the crisis level. Of course, it took months to understand the real reason for the turning point because some relief valves disguised the situation—not to mention "messengers who did not want to be killed." This example explains why narrow-minded financial logic of the past is not always prudent today.

If you run a shop where you use enforced quotas or progressively difficult piece rates that keep laborers just above some minimal production level, you had better hope none of your competitors undertake a modern way of managing. Fatigue and disgust are causing your employees to offer little advice on improving the processes. Every minute is a struggle for them. I heard one say in a meeting, "We have a power struggle here. Management has the power; we have the struggle."

Expecting employees to force a system to perform beyond its capabilities is a major source of fear. I have seen dozens of cases where removing the quotas not only reduced apprehension, but increased creativity. Furthermore, unexpected, immediate short-term increases in production resulted.

For some, this new approach (away from numerical quotas) could elicit unpredictable results. You, therefore, don't change the management methods abruptly without first enlightening the frontliners about the Deming vision. If you do this pretraining, the workers will see to it that the new method works in order to "keep the *by-the-numbers* monkey off our backs." Although management may doubt it, the frontliners want to make more money for the company. They want more productivity, and generally for unselfish reasons. They have 80 percent of the answers to the problems; managers and staff engineers have the remaining 20 percent. Put these two groups together and the synergy yields 150 percent of what you ever dreamed of. This isn't an idle statement; I have witnessed it many times.

To reiterate, the employees can't bulldoze a stable system beyond its natural capabilities without losing profits. Without system improvements by management, this struggle will lead to forgone earnings. With numerical quotas, you'll either nudge the employees down a quick path to burnout or sanction complacency because everyone can beat the rate. When you expect too much, the punishment is frequently a delayed action through a relief valve. Someone else gets the blame. Only system improvements by upper management can stop this. This may be strong talk, but it's true. Tightwads do not get discouraged: The actions warranted by management are normally only procedural, and free in terms of out-of-pocket costs. Deming warned against "throwing money at problems foolishly hoping they will go away and not return to your desk."

As a review: For the stable system, only management can eliminate the elusive system problems. What about the other situation: the *unstable system*—the cases where the bell does not reveal a random roulette wheel with unchanging odds. These erratic situations typically stand out as emergencies, and the frontline employees can usually deal with these local faults. Our basic problem exists because we don't know what to do when there are no emergencies.

When someone does the statistical analysis properly—a charting of the roulette wheel occurrences—you find to your surprise that ninety-eight percent of the processes out there are *in control.* Thus, there is no crisis. Don't let the common-cause aberrations lead you to knee jerks. One approach to "solving problems when there is no emergency" is the totally empowered interdepartmental team. These teams have not caught on well yet. Yes, every firm has its teams; but management often has not empowered them, and sometimes for good reasons. Few companies understand how to run the teams. Review the References or appendix A for suggestions.

Organizations, like people, are prisoners of habit—that which we do repeatedly. Achieving organizations, however, are constantly finding better ways. For them the "quo has lost its status." A related point by Deming recommends you add *continual improvement* to each worker's job description. I agree (almost). First, there are a few necessary paper-shuffling

jobs—and dull people who have gravitated toward them—
that offer no chance of improvement. But there are a very
few. I estimate the percentage of your jobs you must initially
exclude in the press for continual improvement to be about
ten percent, and this should decrease every year. The employees, however, know about these jobs and people. Some folks
will forever only be able to respond to the work before them
on their desks. Therefore, in large meetings you must not
globally espouse the thrust toward continual improvement
for all people without acknowledging a few possible exceptions. You can plant the seed in a global meeting, but follow-
up is a one-on-one issue. Still, be careful with this drive for
demonstrated continual improvement. This is not a first step.
You can't and must not ask employees to overcome single-
handedly the very system problems that drained their spirits.
Premature pie-in-the-sky, numerical wishes will make the situation worse.

You must learn to celebrate even the smallest sustainable
improvements as you move away from the old approach—
espousing numerical goals and later returning to be the
"judge" to audit whether people met expectations.   (If the
power to judge excites you, please get a hold of yourself. Your
Hollywood-infested world is about to crumble.)

Real achievement can't exist without expectations, but I
would not ask for continual improvement in a formal way until
about seventy-five percent of the contents of this book are in
place, and also not until management has empowered and
funded people to make progress. How would this apply to the
mail sorters in the previous example? Ask them to form an
empowered interdepartmental team and to first discuss with
management the team's modus operandi. And then, after
weeks of brainstorming, they must present a ranked list of
action items. (Follow appendix A *exactly*.) The team's goal
would be to show a statistically significant improvement every
half-year from then on. That's all. There is no pass-fail numerical goal. We'll take anything we can get. It's time to "sweat
the little stuff" and open the faucet to a constant flow of

improvement recommendations in the future—ones that management implements with no cherry picking. The front-line workers have had it with *"I'll get back to you on that"* and then no follow-through. (The "suggestion faucet" is turned off forever when the manager later introduces and takes credit for the employee's earlier recommendation, to which he had responded, *"I'll get back to you on that."* This has already happened in most organizations.)

If management isn't ready to follow the teams' suggestions without analysis-paralysis, don't ask for large-scale continual improvement. A word of encouragement: The ranked list of action items isn't as scary as it at first seems. Cost is one of the ranking factors. Funding these lists never seems to be a problem.

Executing Deming's ideas reduces stress and fear. It is conceivable that complacency could set in. However, I have not seen that happen. In case it does, management has to be ready to challenge the employees in new ways. Management attitude becomes more important. This is one reason why it is becoming increasingly difficult for some grouchy, poker-faced managers to be successful with subordinates. Along similar lines, total quality management coordinators, Deming facilitators, and the like must have an extraordinary bedside manner. Someone who is a blend of Alan Alda, Phil Donahue, and Oprah Winfrey would do. These charismatic people are in extremely short supply. If upper management does not fit this mold, they must find someone who does and stand by him every step of the way.

After-the-fact, by-the-numbers management is like looking over your shoulder to find out where you've been. It is a way of staying in the past; Deming likened it to a bird flying backwards. In contrast, when the Deming philosophy takes hold, pride of workmanship, attention to prevention, and analysis of root causes prevail.

At this stage of understanding of the Deming philosophy, many say, "We do not use ranking performance appraisals. We do not use numerical management by objectives. We do not manage by fear. But we are not profitable. It looks like the Deming philosophy cannot help us." This, in a few rare instances, may be true. My findings have always been different, however. If profitability is too low, yet the top three deadly diseases are not present, major opportunities usually revolve around these two strategies:

1. Increasing employees' knowledge of the basic theory of our business—the subject of several of Deming's other diseases and points will be covered later. Employees frequently simply do not know what to do or how to do it, but are afraid to ask after they have been in the job for many months. Almost always they do not fully understand how their actions affect people in departments other than theirs. They cover up their ignorance.

2. Improving enthusiasm—the drive to hustle. The remaining Deming principles can help fix some of the loss of morale. People are not as tough as the characters we see in the movies. Our personal agendas have often demoralized them. How many times have I heard frontliners say, "I told them once. I'm not going to say it again"? Dr. Deming's ideas, over time, will mend some of this indifference.

Elimination of the by-the-numbers disease is not a one-shot undertaking. Old habits stick like "super glue" to your fingers. Management must continually scrutinize their actions. For example, I know a manager who has ineffectively tried to stop managing by the numbers by discontinuing the formal management-by-objectives program. He still, however, requires all plant managers to call him every morning to tell if they met their budgeted production quantity the day before. If they did not, they have to explain why, and often get a lecture. The evils of managing by the numbers still eat into their profit margin. Dozens of expensive knee jerks happen every day as the plant employees try to keep their immediate boss out of trouble. About one-third of the plant's accounting activity involves getting ready for this counterproductive call to corporate headquarters. No one wants to tell the big boss about the cost of his demands. (*Note:* Almost everyone counts their money too often, even when there are cash-flow problems. This reveals too much bureaucracy and not enough root-cause problem solving.) At this plant, there is no energy left for long-lasting improvements. They use all their creativity and energy "to play the numbers game," while many real issues are begging for their attention. I know; I have been there.

CHAPTER 8

People *Do* Work for the Money

Some misquote Deming as being against incentive pay. Deming abhorred individual piece rates and per-unit pay based on a single, potentially suboptimal measure. However, any form of profit sharing based on a composite dimension is usually good. The global incentive should be the same percentage for everybody, include all employees, and encompass quality, service, quantity, etc. (It is best to use three-period moving averages as the basis for calculation so there is no pressure to sacrifice the next cycle.)

Money is a motivator, but not as it seems. If people perceive their pay to be unfair or below industry (community) averages, they seek employment elsewhere. That is why psychologists call pay a maintenance factor. It can "maintain" your presence, and that's about it. Superior corporate performance comes through the intrinsic motivation of pride of workmanship. A good group incentive can add to this enthusiasm.

Deming considered the so-called "pay for performance," based on a ranking performance appraisal system, a most ruinous disease. My experience has convinced me he was right. "Pay for performance" has a nice ring to it, but it is one of those cases where a good catchphrase can hide for fifty years the need to analyze what it really means. The aims are teamwork and synergies. We do not want internal competition for a few hundred dollars more in this year's raise, which boosts a few people's egos at the expense of the masses through a ranking performance appraisal system. With team-work the pie can be bigger for everyone.

On a related subject, salesmen operating out in the field can be team players and still be on commission, if we pay attention. (This is the only place where Deming and I dis-agree.) These "road warriors," out there in the company cars, watching cable TV in lonely hotel rooms, and risking their paychecks on a fickle economy, are a different breed from the on-site workers. Unlike many office dwellers, taking risks and being financially rewarded for it motivates most salesmen. They work isolated out on the road, and the other employ-ees back home don't perceive that we have to take dollars away from someone else when we pay these salesmen larger commissions.

Power and prestige motivate people differently. A few chief-tains will sacrifice the long-term to reach a short-term numer-ical quota. They believe that if they look good enough, they can in some cases quickly move up or out to greener pastures. No wonder Deming listed *mobility of management* as one of the deadly diseases. Management must make sure the boss watch-ers don't get preferential treatment. In the most profitable companies I see today there is an "anti-sucking-up" culture. (Let the professional "ladder climbers" go someplace else to "look pretty.")

Few mobile administrators can switch industries and suc-cessfully run all kinds of businesses. That is because the "nuts and bolts" are more important than any management theo-ries, by a factor of about a million. The concept of the uni-versal manager is dwindling. (Some exceptions exist, I suppose, at the very top—where mingling with Wall Street is more important than nurturing the company's processes and products.)

Bringing in new managers is risky. They import deadly

diseases; they feel pressured to boss-watch to justify their existence; they may not match the culture. The concept of "needing new blood" is as outdated as blood-letting to cure infections. The object nowadays is zero unplanned turnover through the types of things listed below. You can add at least a dozen of your own:

Parallel career paths for technical specialists. Expecting everyone to progress through the management ranks elicits boss watching and burnout.

Create a succession plan. There's no excuse for promoting from the outside, starting five years from today's date.

Base salaries on community averages and an understandable formula for cost-of-living raises. Try to please everyone—especially the squeaking wheels—and you can expect constant employee turnover. The good ones that have options often leave; the others stay.

Budget five days per year for seminar attendance for everyone.

Use flex-time when possible.

Dismiss or relocate people-punishing managers. I can't understand why even the people above them are afraid of these guys!

CHAPTER 9

Cease Dependence on Mass Inspection—Strive for Less After-the-Fact Appraisal

Policemen catch people doing things wrong after the fact. Nurturing parents stop crime in a preventive way. Which is more cost effective? There's a parallel in management. After-the-fact appraisal or auditing as a widespread management practice is a flag highlighting the potential for a better approach. I see this flag in most troubled companies I visit. It is usually a symptom, as much as a cause.

This related point has two parts: (1) don't depend on mass inspection, and (2) strive for less after-the-fact appraisal.

The first part pertains more to manufacturing than to service. The old manufacturing strategy Deming identified years ago in American and European factories involved:

> Making batches as fast as possible with little or no examination
> Collecting the items into lots for inspection purposes
> Inspecting a small fraction of each batch to decide whether to release, scrap, or sort it

Most of us know now this does not work, but this is new-found knowledge. In 1974 Ford had to rework more than eighty percent of the cars leaving the assembly line. Now this percentage is close to zero. There are no more numerical quotas that a supervisor's ranked performance appraisal depends upon. An operator can slow or stop the line after he inspects

his own work. In the old days the quality assurance department's job was "not to let any bad lots get out of here," as they
used to say. People infrequently looked "upstream" to prevent
defects. Most people thought—incorrectly—that scant, after-
the-fact "screening" guaranteed sufficient quality. The main
reason for this misconception was that the Department of
Defense seemed to sanction this method through its military
standards for contractor compliance. These lot-acceptance
plans were "thrown together" during World War II as stopgap
measures, intentionally designed not to obstruct many ship-
ments. No one ever intended them to be in use for the next
fifty years. (I will spare you the 200-page statistical proof that
shows that any after-the-fact, lot-acceptance quality assurance
plan does not provide the parts-per-million quality required in
today's marketplace—it does not even come close to it.)

A complacency that accompanies acceptance sampling is
the failure to look upstream. All lot-acceptance plans allow a
lofty percentage of defective items to reach the customer at
times. This despicable proportion is often one percent. Do
you want your TV to operate only 99 times in a 100?

In defense of those still using lot-acceptance sampling
plans, they rarely do so out of gross ignorance. Either the
process is so new there are no "upstream windows" to look
into for controlling quality at its source, or subsequent in-
house processing automatically culls out the defects before
the ultimate customer sees them. Still, this is an expensive way
to go that ideally should be stopped.

The second similar part of this point pertains to "striving
for less after-the-fact appraisal"—something closely related
to the by-the-numbers disease. You can't efficiently "inspect"
quality into a product or service. The outdated "make-inspect-
correct" cycle will assure your demise in today's marketplace.
Some types of audits apply here also. Punitive inspections may
be the only way to get some people to "do right" at the
moment. This means, however, that deep-rooted problems
exist. Sometimes you can find them.

Prevention is the only way to generate top profitability. Do not waste all your energy trying to spot problems already there. Instead, look for root causes and make the following types of after-the-fact, appraisal situations unnecessary:

• Accountants having to closely inspect all travel expense vouchers
• Trip reports for routine business travel
• Accounting variance reports used by people who have no concept of the roulette wheel
• Time clocks
• Budgets with no preventive plan for reducing expenses
• Ridiculously low approval limits for department managers
• Supervisor approval required before work leaves the department
• Signatures required from layers of administrators

We can't discontinue most of the above practices abruptly. But as Deming brought to the forefront, the needs for these types of procedures are symptoms of more basic root problems somewhere. For an example, needing to get layers of management signatures is, in some cases, a result of the front-line workers not having sufficient knowledge of the extended process. The root problem is that we have exposed too few people to operations outside their department.

Today, the excuse, "Oops, we made a mistake," is being replaced by root-cause analysis and preventive thinking. When I get involved with a client who has troublesome quality problems, I always try to look further upstream than he has before. The reasons often surface. And the answer is *never* to apply a larger dose of whatever "medicine" they are taking. What is needed is a new "prescription." We can no longer stopgap problems by adding people, job positions, and clumsy procedures to treat symptoms. Causes must be eliminated.

CHAPTER 10

Strive for More Constancy of Purpose

Lack of *constancy of purpose*—This is the most pervasive and global of Deming's diseases and points. For that reason, some people start here when beginning the transformation. But lack of constancy of purpose is also the most confusing of Deming's points and diseases, and starting with it may impede progress for years. You need to be six months into your transition before you start talking about this concept.

Constancy of purpose is the continual striving to be in business for the long haul, and the desire to base all policies, operating procedures, and decisions toward this end. Another definition of constancy of purpose is "everybody pulling in the same direction." You have constancy of purpose when the answer to the question, "Why are we in business?" is *not* "to make money," but something more definitively related to a local mission statement. The statement "to make money" isn't specific enough and offers little guidance. A mission statement must provide direction, not platitudes or vague comments that sound like motherhood and apple pie. Consider this good mission statement for a chemical company:

> The mission of XYZ company is to be the first on the market with chemicals tailor-made for each customer, and to anticipate their needs for the future. We will direct all actions toward better service, increasing pride of workmanship, and minimizing product variability from some

target. Simply staying in specification is not enough. We will find a way to eliminate any reasons why a customer could possibly not like doing business with us.

Regardless what you do about Deming's points and diseases, fifteen percent of the "diseased" managers won't convert to a more enlightened approach. Use the mission statement to control them and to make sure they are *aware of the consequences* of continuing their outdated practices.

A comment I overheard from an innovative plant manager ten years ago illustrates constancy of purpose and the long-term orientation. He made it in response to a broken component:

"Okay, Bill, the pump is malfunctioning again. Do whatever you have to do to fix it. Come back into my office when you get it going. I want to know what projects you are working on this week that will guarantee our survival and productivity five years from now."

This became the "question of the month" around the plant as the boss began to direct some attention to the long term. He believed the short term gets fixed; what's important is focusing on the future. As you would expect, chaos erupted at first. People had to hustle and learn to be creative. Today, ten years later, people often ask this former plant manager (now an executive vice-president) why this particular plant is still in a class by itself and worldwide. He always says: "It was what we did ten years ago." Now that's constancy of purpose! Can we have it when the focus is short-term numerical quotas and boss watching, and when the administrators are mobile managers? A philosophical manager told me once, "The years teach a great deal the days never know." *Things go wrong* when the management expectations don't support this philosophy.

CHAPTER 11

Do Not Throw the New-Hires to the Wolves

New-hires raise a troublesome—but easily fixable—issue because of the half-hearted training it is so tempting to offer them. Deming included this as one of his points because he detested the way many firms rely almost solely upon on-the-job training (OJT) as an instructional tool for new-hires, especially the salaried ones. OJT is never sufficient. Workers training workers with no formal guidelines leads to problems. They pass misconception on; they recommend jury rigs; they seldom provide the why; ad nauseam. The dread of future competition for promotions can also prevent cooperation among the trainees and ones designated to "show them the ropes."

For those of us who get around to many companies, the consequences of poor initial training are evident. Working with multiple-crew (location) companies, I have almost always found that no one group has the equivalent perception of the same job, or a sufficient knowledge of the total operation. Each has a small piece—enough to get by. Taking best practices from each group and formulating a detailed training guide (for new-hires and old-timers) yields unheard of profits. Granted, it takes management finesse to overcome the not-invented-here syndrome.

Often I have found that this problem is a result of upper management having chosen to delegate the training responsibilities to frontline workers rather than dealing with it themselves. While delegation of responsibilities may be management's natural inclination, it does not make for smart business sense. An employee who is taught his duties and responsibilities as well as how his piece of the puzzle fits into the entire picture is more likely to be an asset.

Another issue: Can you begin to see how the personal agendas resulting from ranking performance appraisals or suboptimal departmental quotas can lead to employees selfishly showing no interest in training new arrivals? The various parts of the Deming philosophy reinforce each other. If you're not beginning to see this, take an incubation break from this book. Reflect back on the previous chapters.

People who do well in organizations are usually the ones who are astute and lucky enough to have a nurturing sponsor and personal training. Why not assign each new-hire a senior sponsor whose own performance we grade by the success of the novice? (Obviously, you must involve the sponsor in the hiring.) Do not leave this to chance. Don't play the game of seeing which new employee is strong enough to survive. If you do, a few will endure and progress up the ladder. Most will wither and hide it, some to the point of becoming deadweight—to be demolished in the next downsizing.

Experienced employees who will not volunteer for this training duty, in my opinion, need some additional nurturing in being a team player. This is in contrast to their being a career-climber at the expense of the long-term profitability of the firm.

Along with this, someone in authority must make sure the newcomer gets training in the following, and in a formal way:

The organization structure and how work gets done.

The culture and company values.

Deming theory and how it applies to their new job. (We don't want new-hires to import diseases.)

The extended process. Let new workers spend a few days with a customer, a salesman, a major supplier, etc. Have them work in all major departments under a carefully chosen trainer.

The theoretical aspects of the job. As an example, if you run a hospital, show the results of focus groups or marketing research on why patients or doctors most frequently change care facilities.

Your own list will be longer. Each newcomer needs a checklist that a sponsor monitors. Don't take chances. If you do, expect things to go wrong.

When a person is in the job market, often something is wrong with his old ways or, more likely, with his earlier situation. At a minimum, he never figured out how to get along with his last boss, or he has no experience (right out of school). In any event, don't let his shortcomings get repeated.

CHAPTER 12

Consider People Already on the Job Need More Training

Many mistakes arise from a lack of knowledge. Some errors follow as a delayed response to our inadequate training of new-hires. After a period of time on the job, people won't stand up and say, "Help me; I don't know how to do my job." Do not expect many experienced employees to risk looking stupid by asking for additional basic training.

Trial-and-error training has many shortcomings—some technical, many psychological. It is common to find innovative firms allocating two to three percent of the employees' time retraining on items like the ones below:

The extended process.

Deming training. Some up-front visionary training by a master is a necessity.

The basic theory. I have a technique as a consultant that is like "picking up manna from the factory floor." Across all crews or people doing a job (maybe at different locations), I identify who is best at which tasks. Then I let them train each other.

Problem-solving tools. They need this, but be careful. Anything that seems to fit everywhere to a trainer probably applies "well" nowhere.

Statistical training. I almost didn't include this item because we professional statistical trainers have done such a poor job previously. Briefly, some problems included: too much too soon, not enough, using a shotgun instead of a rifle, no company examples, little follow-through, an egghead trainer, and more. See the References for a few good basic texts.

You add more items. It will take one to three years to improve employee retraining, but it will be worth it. The Motorola company, as an example, claims a 35-to-1 payback ratio on their retraining efforts, which involves about 5 percent of the employees' time. There are many challenges ahead: I read that for leadership positions, we'll have to assimilate the equivalent of a college degree every seven years to keep up.

You can't fail as an instructor if you remember what a mentor told me: "Teaching should be full of ideas, not simply stuffed with facts."

CHAPTER 13

Institute Leadership

Deming told us that supervision is in need of an overhaul, but he didn't tell us how to do it. I do have a few observations—a very few.

The first: Managers who have strong needs for control and power, or who want others to revere them for their position, are going to be frustrated in the future. People are no longer willing to tolerate them—whether they are right or wrong. Empowerment is being cast upon us by those on the frontline like the sea upon the shore. In several organizations that have taken the lead in empowerment, the supervisors tell me they now feel as if they work for the subordinates, compared to the old situation where the employees answered to them. I think this is what Dr. Deming had in mind.

Traditional forms of management honor stability, systems of control, and procedures (the files). Furthermore, a conservative, detached style and behavior seem to fit their stereotype. Conventional executives are managers, but we now need leaders. Managers concern themselves with the control of resources and making things happen by giving orders. Leadership is harder. It involves establishing credibility and trust with their enthusiasm and deeds. Without this in the future, expect *things to go wrong.*

Supervisory people need some training, that's for sure. However, the Deming philosophy is not the thing you can have taught to them—the panacea pill—that will solve all of your problems while you get on with *your* agenda. Some firms precede any sort of new approach with supervisory training, and often seem to stop there with the hope that it will "get the issue off my desk." This does not take hold for many reasons you already know about. Don't let the same thing happen with your Deming transition. Let the supervisors see higher management taking initiative for the first year or more on the things you have just read about. Deming said supervisors must become coaches, not order-givers. I suppose it is okay to tell them this, but be prepared to work with them one-on-one during their difficult transition. (I do believe, however, first-line supervisors need to be among the first to receive vision-ary Deming training, but they should not be the initial group expected to take action. Let them read this book instead.)

I often encounter anxious supervisors whose jobs, to them, seem insecure because of the empowerment of their subor-dinates. Their management has often tried to smooth the transition by saying, "You are now a facilitator, project man-ager, and problem solver." This well-intended statement has frequently not helped. Management defined their jobs as order-giver and checker many years ago, and the empower-ment phenomenon sneaked up on the supervisors and their bosses. Hopefully, this has not happened to your firm. Start now with supervisory training on project management, or with reassignment. You need a two-year lead time.

Another idea I have seen work: Create an *advance* list of detailed projects for each supervisor—tailor-made for his interests. This gives him something to do to replace the time void from not having to personally supervise employees.

CHAPTER 14

Break Down Barriers between Departments

Accomplishing the previous points will help to break down departmental barriers. Abolishing ranking performance appraisals and the elimination of suboptimal departmental quantitative objectives will be a good start, but management must do more. I know a division manager who bases all qualitative performance appraisals and promotion decisions on one thing: how well his people work as team members. (They also do written peer reviews.) He says the routine work gets done—out of pride and an *awareness of the consequences.* But breaking down departmental barriers won't happen on its own. We must take overt action to solve the system problems in the "white spaces" of the organizational chart. (Interdepartmental teams will help nourish this transition.)

I think Deming included this point as a constant reminder that decisions and policies must, at a minimum, not heighten the walls between departments. We need this constant reminder. Our stopgap response to many problems is often to departmentalize further so we can hold one guy accountable "when this happens again." (But this is bureaucratic overmanagement.) Of course, this is necessary every eon or so, but as the Deming philosophy progresses and the departmental lines get fuzzy, some bureaucrats will squawk. Learn not to listen. The Deming transition makes companies more profitable and the work more satisfying; but managing isn't necessarily easier during the transition. There are no quick-fixes.

The beginning of your list of "things to do" to tear down departmental barriers:

1. Reverse performance appraisals. These help prevent a boss from instilling the fear of "Your job is to make me look good!" What is implied by that type of message is "Forget about other departments and the total good of the firm."

2. Upon the retirement or separation of a manager whose main job has been coordination, always consider reorganizing to eliminate the job. This forces the destruction of departmental walls.

3. Use first names only.

4. Counsel excessive memo writers. Writing memos is usually an outdated practice.

5. There should be no dress code differentiating managers from doers. Business suits look good, but at times force an unnecessary hierarchial barrier. *Prediction:* In a hundred years pictures of men wearing coats and ties will look as weird as Thomas Jefferson's wig, or Ghengis Khan's hairdo.

6. Destroy the organization chart. "Too complex to do without" implies that it is too complex to be profitable.

7. Eliminate executive dining rooms, washrooms, prestige parking, etc. When I see these, I sell my stock in this company. These, however, are symptoms, not causes.

8. Use peer performance reviews across departmental boundaries. This is a tough pill to swallow. Those who can't handle it will likely "wash out" during the Deming transition anyway. It will take several cycles to see the good effect of this. Be patient.

9. Create a cross-training orientation program for the new-hires and the most experienced workers.

The outdated feeling of line managers, "This is my turf! How dare you try to tell me how I'm going to run it," must be abolished. Over time, departmental managers must lose their veto power of brilliant staff ideas. Granted, much of the improved coordination must come from the staff specialists. Through improved training on the extended process and nurturing from upper management, the staff people can learn to coordinate better with line management up-front. Then the loss of veto power will not seem so drastic.

CHAPTER 15

Do Not Rest on Your Laurels— Get Moving

The order in which Deming listed the points in his own books was confusing to many managers; the lead-in items at the beginning of his roster included the vaguest concepts. I have already reordered his list and have anchored the top with clear-cut "things to do." Here is the end of my slate.

His point #14: *Take action to accomplish the plan.* When I first heard this, it sounded to me as if he said, "Okay, I've told you what to do, now do it!" After ten years of thought, I realized this point contains more than an instruction to get going. It reflects Deming's deep understanding of how managers think. They want a roster of "things to do." Embedded in point #14 is the following list:

Start with broad visionary training on the Deming philosophy so people will see what is coming. Surprises elicit unexpected results. This book is at a good level for visionary training. Use examples that come from the company. Generic training has little benefit.

Create interdepartmental teams on some high-priority system problems. My own advice: Don't let someone's personal agenda determine which initial problems you tackle. *A consultant's secret:* In the beginning, choose "sure successes" that impact the bottom line. You must begin on a positive note. (*False starts* are among the obstacles listed in a later chapter.)

Establish cross-functional teams to let everyone determine
who's the customer and what are his needs. In today's competitive environment, the real customer is seldom the boss.

About seventy-five percent of your way through the transition,
have cross-functional teams flow chart the important
processes with the intent of eliminating wasted effort.
Warning: If the company has historically laid off employees with each labor-saving effort, don't waste your time or
risk your credibility by asking the employees once again to
"eliminate themselves."

Deming's Point #2: *Adopt the new philosophy.* It seems as if I
already said this, but I didn't. Here is what Deming wanted
us to constantly have on our minds as we glance at his 14
points, which you might want to frame and put on the wall.

The knee-jerking behavior of some managers does not
always mean they are stupid or insensitive, so don't let pride
prevent you from owning up to your problems and continuing the Deming transition. We learned our profit-draining,
short-term approaches to management between 1950 and
1968 when the competitive conditions were different. Immediately after World War II, the short-term, by-the-numbers
approach worked well for the moment. Before the rest of the
world rebuilt, we owned all of the markets. How could we
have known our future foreign competitors were listening to
Deming (and others) to get ready to encroach on us? Learning under conditions that won't repeat—as during our
monopolistic situation after World War II—is called **supersti-
tious learning.** We were all superstitiously trained (not selfishly half-witted as it often appears) until Deming wrote about
his theories in the early 1980s. Nevertheless, before people
understood him, a lot of "management bashing" took place.
But it was generally unjustified. Managers were not stupid,
just superstitiously trained.

This point #2 has another part. Deming rightly warned
against turning our heads from defects and delays. Although
patience and understanding are the mark of a seasoned

executive, you must ask for continual improvement in quality and productivity. (As mentioned earlier, don't rekindle the deadly diseases when you do this. We must solve everlasting system problems through interdepartmental teams.) This requires planning and action. You can't simply ask for better financial results; alternatively you should expect your subordinates to present their plans for improving. This transition toward higher expectations is taking place.

As an example of our newfound impatience with shabby quality, in 1970 I was willing to take my new car back to the dealer four or five times to get the bugs out and then buy the same model from him three years later when the car died at 50,000 miles. Now, I expect *no* defects when the car is new and only minimal repairs for 125,000 miles. Customers are now like Oscar Wilde, who said, "I have the simplest of tastes. I'm easily satisfied with the best."

CHAPTER 16

Profound Knowledge

Dr. Deming's last contribution was his concept of **profound knowledge**. He often commented, and I agree, that we manage our firms in a regimented, myopic, and uncreative way. Because I have already covered most of the profound knowledge, I have kept this chapter short. Read, reread, and memorize these next few pages. It overlaps the rest of his theory, so don't get confused when you feel you have seen some of this.

A few people are enlightened by nature. However, for most of us, according to Deming, achieving profound knowledge will add new meaning to your life and instill a desire to teach others the "new way." If this does not to happen to you, perhaps you don't understand yet.

There are four interrelated parts to the concept of profound knowledge: appreciation for the system, the concept of variation, the theory of knowledge, and psychology.

A SYSTEM

For near-optimum performance, the parts of a system must reinforce each other, not compete against one another. For example, the listeners judge an orchestra, not the illustrious players. Similarly, a firm's travel department can save money by getting rock-bottom fares that require travelers to stay over

Saturday night or connect through Chihuahua, Mexico, at 2 A.M., but the passengers become frazzled and demoralized. Who wins? The travel department's egos. Who loses? Everybody else. Net result? Less profitability.

Top money-making companies benefit from the 2+2=5 synergistic effects. They pay attention in hundreds of ways. Ranking performance appraisals, not considering the extended process, ignoring the need to cross-train, suboptimizing numerical objectives, failing to nurture new-hires, etc., are *never* among these ways.

Through cross-training (point #13), people begin to learn that every decision affects all parts of the system. Management must dampen the internal competition through their actions and every breath they take.

VARIATION

Remember the example of the time it takes to service a customer? Variation is a fact of life. A stable system is one whose roulette wheel and bell curve show a random variation around the average over time. Only management can improve the stable system. The frontline workers are powerless; there are no local faults. We demoralize people and elicit expensive knee-jerk responses when we treat system variations as local faults and expect the employees to respond to random aberrations. Middle management often fails to present system problems to those above them. They feel this would make them look weak. (John Wayne solved his own problems.)

The roulette wheel in action could show data in an ***enumerative*** fashion. By watching the creation of the bell, you can see what happens over time and theorize about the nature of the problem. The same thing happens if you plot these data on a graph. You learn whether there are mostly system issues or predominantly local faults. You will also be able to see any trends or cycles (peaks or valleys in the bell or lots of blocks on the floor).

On the other hand, one observation, or a few measurements during a fleeting interval is an ***analytical*** study and rarely tells you anything. I worked with a utility company that sent a corporate technocrat to ride with a repairman for a *single* day to do a so-called work sampling. The technician made six comparatively simple service calls that day. The new daily quota became *six*. Few could meet it. This *analytical* "snapshot" was not valid. Some days are worse than average; some counties cover more miles. Relief valves erupted. Technicians had to leave repair jobs undone to move on to other calls to meet their daily quota. The cost was in the millions, but management never understood the root cause. My contact within the company knew that management "killed messengers" and also knew nothing about frontline services. He, therefore, would not tell the company heads about this profound knowledge. Instead, the utility company instituted a rate hike, which the customers are still paying.

Deming said, "A system can't correct itself. Improvement must come from the outside." I'm afraid he is correct, at least for several more years. Personal agendas, departmental boundaries, by-the-numbers thinking, boss watching, etc., prevent reflective thinking and creativity until the Deming transition takes hold.

Let me illustrate this with an analogy. Field biologists use the phrase *search image* to explain their focus. If you have a search image for monkeys in the jungle, you'll see them; otherwise, you may not. Outside consultants and internal change agents (who take time for reflective thinking and thought incubation) have a search image for process improvements. Unfortunately, we often peg insiders who creatively evaluate everything as wave makers. We don't allow them to "play in the reindeer games." Furthermore, people who are both courageous and creative often say aloud what others would only think to themselves. This elicits weird glances, which most of us fear. Employees react to anxiety and further ego-smashing by learning how to fit in.

The Deming transition spreads the attaboys more evenly

across the organization—where they belong—making it tough for some selfish insiders to have the motivation to accomplish the total effort. It will be many years before your newfound Deming objectivity drastically reduces the internal struggle for an ever-decreasing number of promotions. Everybody still "wants the credit." A good, unselfish consultant can circumvent this conflict. Not by taking all the credit, but from adhering to the words of Dr. Joe Mullins: "You can accomplish anything you want as long as you let someone else take the credit."

THEORY OF KNOWLEDGE

I heard once that experience is a ruthless teacher. It gives the test before presenting the lesson. Deming expanded my thinking when he said, "Without a theory, experience has no meaning. Information is not the same as knowledge." A dictionary contains information, but no knowledge. (There's no fool like an old fool. He got the same one day's experience over and over. He had no theories or generalizations to test or to organize his findings.) Numbers on a page comprise information; an understanding of the roulette wheel leads to knowledge. Then come the questions: What knowledge? Are there any trends or cycles? Is the system stable, which means only management can impart lasting improvements (the theory)?

Theory is the "window to the world." It enables managers to predict, to generalize, and to evaluate situations as they gather new knowledge, rather than only responding to the latest emergency. It takes repeated observations to verify a theory—and most importantly, the will to explore. However, only one unexpected result can nullify or alter a theory. (It may seem weird, but it's true. I'll spare you the philosophical statistical proof.) However, we often do not address opportunities the way Deming recommended.

The scientific approach, which has led to every important

development we enjoy today, revolves around formulating a theory and objectively testing it. But managers frequently shun this creative method for self-serving reasons. Perhaps they do this because of the male ego. And women have simply copied the behavior that results from this detrimental testosterone influence. Managers often go to all extremes to prove their initial notions to be correct, versus subjecting them to impartial testing. A defensive manager who often did this told me there was much boss watching, politicking, and bureaucratic butt-covering paperwork that stole his time. He only had the energy to posit one hypothesis or solution for each problem—versus multiple attempts if the data did not support his first guess. He could not let it be known if the subsequent data proved him wrong. Being incorrect would diminish his credibility among his subordinates. A massive environmental change may help him. Maybe the other parts of the Deming philosophy, which reduce the tendency to boss-watch, would improve his innovativeness. Maybe a firing squad would help.

For example, one of my clients was upset because the employees were not taking the initiative to improve the processes. There were no apparent reasons for this. Upper management had information about the situation, but no "theory" and knowledge as to why it was happening or how to deal with it. I did an enumerative study over time to find that (1) the employees were boss watching with the sole goal of pleasing him; (2) the boss (reluctantly) had to generate almost all the new ideas; (3) risk taking could lead to failures; (4) due to the fear of failure, they missed many creative opportunities; (5) fear existed in everyone's heart; (6) managers had not used fear intentionally in years, and not accidentally in months; (7) promising lifetime employment accomplished nothing; (8) no initiative was being taken—employees were waiting for further orders.

Based on these observations, the knowledge showed that according to my previously mentioned *dead-boss theory*, punitive management's previous use of fear (intentional or not) had coerced the people into their security need level, which resulted in lots of skeletons in the closet.

Consequently, the employees could not respond to recognition until management took overt, bending-over-backwards action to satisfy the thwarted security needs. The managers had to go beyond the call of duty, rather than following normal business practices.

The applicable theory that aided change came from the knowledge that it takes more overt counter-fear action to remove the skeletons from the closet than it did to put them there. Time alone does not heal the wounds. They needed an anti-"who done it" culture. Managers had to evaluate every action based on whether it could possibly instill any fear. (This applies the principles discussed in chapter 4.) The change process took about two years.

Management had been analyzing the symptoms, but until they had a theory, it was difficult to formulate an action plan to remove the cause. It was also difficult not to knee jerk from the latest squeaking wheel. It seemed that stopping their old ways would quickly solve the problem. However, they had to understand the dead-boss theory to improve: It takes overt action, not mere removal of the immediate causative effect, to eliminate the future responses to past fear.

The saying that experience is the best teacher is simply a myth. It is a good instructor, when blended with theory from formal education, reading, or reflective thought—or even better, from all three. Then the synergy can blossom.

PSYCHOLOGY

People are different. There is no way to design a bureaucratic system to motivate them. (These systems can demotivate, however.) Management has to nurture each person individually. In the absence of the deadly diseases, there may be self-imposed *intrinsic* motivation. However, relief valves have hidden the intrinsic motivation of ninety-seven percent of the employees. There is a phrase in anthropology called *participatory mana*—when people "are" what they are doing. We want more people to have participatory mana. Then they will make the firm great. (Many upper managers have this spirit and often cannot understand the working stiffs. Executives do not face the same numbing trivia.) **Extrinsic** motivators, such as money or contests, aren't the answer to lasting superior performance if they in any way promote internal competition. You lose more than you gain, *always*.

Employees expect, and deserve, to participate in the long-term profits through an understandable pay formula; but the American theory of short-term incentives and rewards is bankrupt and has fostered a "mental welfare" in some firms. A steady stream of research has shown that immediate rewards for explicit actions can actually undermine genuine interest and diminish performance over the long haul. "Do this and you'll get that" is not far removed from, "Do this, or else." Place a short-term reward in front of someone and he or she will tend to take the quickest and surest—but not necessarily the most creative—route to that reward. The result is that there is little or no permanent improvement in process or product by the frontline workers. You must hire hordes of managers and engineers to find innovations (most of which are already there, but are suppressed).

Why are carrot-and-stick rewards not effective in the long term? First, the external incentive distracts from the task itself, reducing it to a means to an end; when someone removes the reward, most lose interest in the chore. Second—and the reason most quoted by psychologists—short-term rewards convey the message that the task isn't worth doing for its own sake.

The leader has a responsibility to create an environment within which employees can motivate themselves. In order to accomplish this, Deming gave us many ideas. We cite managers for their attempts to control. We treasure leaders for their example. Remember that sitting in your office, you can find hundreds of ways to create procedures and controls to demotivate subordinates. If you're thoughtful, there may be a few ways you can eliminate barriers that are robbing them of their intrinsic motivation. There are precious few ways you can create new motivation from behind your desk (of any lasting consequence). When God created the human psyche, he cursed management. We have a powerful capability to demotivate, but a minimal proficiency to create lasting enthusiasm. Notice the above phrases *sitting in your office* and *from behind your desk.* I do believe managers can have an influence by mingling, offering cheerful encouragement, eliciting advice, and showing concern when things are going badly. In other words: get out of the office. This fulfills short-term social needs, and few employees today will support a boss they do not like. Insensitive bureaucrats can seldom inspire others to be competitive in the new-world economy. So *managing by walking around is useful,* but long-term striving for continual improvement, however, must come from within the employees. Most of what you have heard about management—things to make it easy—are simply not true. Leaders can only provide the correct environment and set examples. What do employees want? Try these:

• Eliminate all the deadly diseases.
• Implement the fourteen points.
• Make all the Deming concepts someone's responsibility. There will be dozens of flow charts and lists of "things to do."
• Provide time for reflective thinking.
• Give them a "piece of the collective pie." Make them all internal bean counters.

In summary, Deming's concept of profound knowledge states:

1. All parts of a system are interrelated.

2. Frontline workers can't control the common cause of the roulette wheel. We can only understand a system by analyzing

data over time. A snapshot (the numbers on the page) is misleading.

3. Information does not equal knowledge. Wisdom can only be established by verifying theories. Experience is a bad teacher in the absence of theory.

4. Bureaucratic systems can only demotivate workers. Intrinsic motivation comes from the work itself if there is pride of workmanship. Carrot-and-stick rewards aren't the answer.

This profound knowledge should permeate all your thought processes.

CHAPTER 17

Review

You have just read my condensed version of Deming's monumental *Out of the Crisis*. Now I'm going to reduce my text even further. Memorize these before you begin your firm's transition. Watch the **boldfaced italics** again, carry these pages around in your mind, and let them incubate.

Any operation gives rise to an enormous number of aberrations that the frontline employees can't control economically. They are often forced to respond by jury-rigging, which occasionally meets demand temporarily but also results in the eruption of expensive **relief valves.** We must direct the total effort of the company toward minimizing root causes, thus making the aberrations fewer. A recap:

Point #12: Eliminate ranking performance appraisals to reduce **boss watching** and to improve **pride of workmanship.** This makes the operation more predictable.

Point #8: Drive out fear in every way. This leads to less irrational behavior and a more stable work environment.

Point #10: Eliminate banners and slogans that delay real action. They provide only a temporary sense of having "done something."

Point #4: Move toward sole sourcing to make the *extended process* more predictable.

Point #11: Discontinue the *knee jerking* and the counterproductive stress of managing by the numbers.

Point #5: Make it clear that *continuous improvement* is in everyone's job description—versus meeting a quota or staying out of trouble. We need to help people establish their measurement criteria. (See *The Deming Vision* for a list that illustrates this point.)

Point #3: Discontinue after-the-fact mass inspection (an example of the tail wagging the dog) and replace it with preventive measures.

Point #1: Improve *constancy of purpose* by instituting a specific mission statement.

Points #6 and #13: Increase training to get everyone on the same sheet of music.

Point #7: Supervisors need to learn to facilitate change rather than thwarting employees' reasoning by simply giving orders.

Point #12: Break down barriers between departments so the *system problems* in the white spaces of the organization chart get solved for a change.

Point #14 and #2: Management's vision must "prime the pump."

If, after instituting the transformation, you hear people saying, "Business as usual," your training or enlightenment was bad. People are skeptical of change; people detest being changed. As a response to new "programs" or changes that come along, many people scramble or "batten down the hatches." This is to make sure the *meaningful* parts of their jobs don't get tampered with. In this context, *meaningful* means important, comfortable, easy, time-passing, fun, risk-free, etc. These meanings are in the mind of the employee;

some are good, some bad; but they cling to all of them.

As we implement the *points*, we cure the *diseases.* Personal agendas, politics, and fear take a backseat to objectivity and common sense. One thing does not change—you still have to hustle and pay attention. This especially applies to the *obstacles* listed on the next few pages.

An often-asked question is "Does implementing the Deming philosophy encompass everything a manager has to do to be successful?" The obvious answer is "no." There are thousands of actions that the employees must appropriately take for a firm to be profitable. Luckily, most are common sense. It does seem, however, that at times I get totally "lost in the forest because of the trees," when trying to help a client. I ultimately find that if he or she had been in the Deming mode, the bad situation(s) would never have occurred. Similarly, every time I read someone's summary of how to manage, or what constitutes a good job, it reeks of Deming. As an example, according to an article in the November 1993 issue of *Men's Health,* in a good job:

1. You're held accountable only for those things you can control.
2. You have enough autonomy to do your job.
3. Individualism is respected.
4. Teamwork is more important than internal competition.
5. You trust and respect your boss.
6. Your boss provides you with regular feedback.
7. There are no posters encouraging you to work harder.

CHAPTER 18

The *Obstacles*

"Trouble can be hiding behind every tree." Seasoned executives know this. Deming listed the common obstacles he confronted in implementing the transformation. I have added a few. You will attach several more. Once the top managers grasp the theory and work up an implementation plan, get off-site and brainstorm a list of obstacles. Be prepared to discuss and overcome them as they arise. Better yet, prevent them. Don't get caught off guard.

To me, the obstacles present the chicken or the egg question—which comes first. I believe most of the obstacles are only symptoms, with root causes prowling in the hedges. We all know the Deming transformation revolves around "treating the disease, not the symptoms." A complete transformation through the Deming principles would likely eradicate most of these obstacles—the very stumbling blocks that will make the implementation difficult. That's another catch-22 situation. But you can't wait. Hit the obstacles head-on as you eliminate the root causes over time. Start with the following list.

OBSTACLES TO SUCCESS

1. Failing to announce at the outset this transition is not optional.

2. Expecting *instant pudding*—erroneously thinking everything will happen quickly and easily.

3. Installing *gadgets* rather than addressing the people issues. Gadgets may be mechanical or procedural jury rigs. They avoid the real problems.

4. Searching for exact examples to copy instead of working out your own plan.

5. Poor teaching of statistical methods.

6. Assuming acceptance sampling provides sufficient quality.

7. Assuming the quality control department can assure sufficient quality while the rest of us go about our routine chores and sometimes tranquilizing ourselves with trivia.

8. Assuming "our problems lie with the work force." The frontline workers are the *most* interested in quality and productivity. Their security depends on it. Never forget this.

9. False starts—not enough advance planning through team efforts.

10. The supposition that "it is only necessary to meet specifications." Can you put a specification on continuous improvement?

11. Inadequate testing of prototypes.

12. Believing outside experts can't help. Thinking outside experts can solve our problems with no involvement by management.

13. Failing to make it clear up-front that the Deming transition won't lead to any "pink slips." If a downsizing is necessary, don't begin with the Deming concepts until everyone knows the layoffs are over. (They know this because you told them.)

14. Upper management must participate, not dictate.

CHAPTER 19

A Few Words Worthy of a Chapter

If accomplished properly, the Deming transition can be disruptive to misguided bureaucrats. *Beware:* Many of them are articulate and can present seemingly good arguments for their half-witted thoughts. It can wear you down, too. They can compress the most words into the smallest thought. *Hence:* the phrase *articulate incompetent*. The more the company needs it, the more uncomfortable the transition can be and the faster their mouths move.

As Deming told us, the transition is not for the timid. Many managers promote tranquillity at all costs. They foolishly see this as their caretaker responsibility. Obviously, these folks can't lead your Deming transition, but they may be able to follow it with a slight kick in the pants.

Your first step is to let all players read this book (or one like it). The next move is to conduct a half-day visionary training session. Announce the elimination of the ranking performance appraisal system at this time. Plant the seeds for what's to come. Everyone needs to see this transition coming weeks before it begins. Have a team make a to-do list with who "carries the ball" for each item. There are only five relevant diseases and fourteen points. But if you look closely, you will see that these result in at least thirty major projects (not 14+5=19), and more than a hundred minor projects. (Be careful not to replace diseases with different afflictions. This is what the bureaucrats like to do.) Also identify and neutralize the obstacles. Establish expectations, but allow twice the time it looks like it will take. Constantly get off-site and evaluate your actions against the theory. Tolerate no compromises.

As you get into this, you will see that doing business now—by paying attention to the basics—just makes more sense. The removal of departmental "walls," personal agendas, boss watching, ignorance, etc., will mean that more effort goes to the bottom line—like in your grandfather's days, before things got so complicated.

Some managers are authorized only to say "no" to a new approach. Others higher up can say "yes or no" to a better way. Of course, unfortunately, many can say nothing at all—the paper shufflers. The message in this book *must* get to the people who can say "yes." I hope that the language has been diplomatic enough for you to recommend the book to a potential "yes"-sayer.

During the editing of this book, Dr. Deming died. I hope we can continue his transition. Asked once how he would be remembered, he said, "If at all, . . . as someone who spent his life trying to keep America from committing suicide." I believe his remarks are right on the money. As an insider, it is difficult for you to see the weirdness of your firm's ways clearly—eventually, most anything makes sense. (Your subconscious will often force you to fit in even when you do not want to.) Following Deming's advice will solve problems you do not even know you have. People have covered them up. History books and movies have cultured Americans "not to complain." For example, the Continental Army toughed it out at Valley Forge, even though food supplies were not far away. So don't complain.

Send me a note and I'll mail you a batch of promotional pamphlets to help you spread the Deming word.

Every time it incorrectly seems that the Deming transition is ho-hum, "business as usual," read this book again. An annual reread for five years is a must.

Thanks for letting me enlighten you.

Epilogue

This book or any of those listed in the References is not intended to make it unnecessary to read Deming's book, *Out of the Crisis,* or another of my books, *The Deming Vision.* It all began with Deming himself and will never die.

The Interdepartmental Team

At least for the next five years it will take interdepartmental teams to bypass the bureaucracy and politics when solving complex interdepartmental system problems. Implementing the Deming philosophy will eventually remove most departmental barriers, boss watching, and personal agendas. For now, however, we need practice working creatively together, which is different from politicking and stroking each other's egos. Interdepartmental teams will provide these rehearsals. The interdisciplinary nature of system problems also necessitates these teams.

From my experience, it is necessary to follow the guidelines below *exactly*. Any other version tailor-made to someone's political orientations will likely be unsuccessful. How do I know? I have been on 200-300 of these teams. Believe it or not, we have been 100 percent successful. (But there have always been great difficulty and back-tracking.) Start with 2-3 teams on projects sure to succeed, but still important to the bottom line. We must see some up-front success. Within a year, you may have 8-10 teams at each installation. People will eventually say, "I am on so many teams, I do not have time to do my job." You will say, "This is your new job. Let's identify some unnecessary trivia in your daily activities that can be eliminated."

Use these fifteen guidelines to fight off the bureaucrats who say, "But this is so different!"

1. We solve system problems only by doing *something different*. Always.

2. People who consider it their sole job to make the boss look good, to advance their careers, or to snatch a larger share of the resources for their department, cannot be on the teams. (Sorry, take your toys and play in somebody else's yard. You don't fit in anymore.)

3. The perennial "pain in the ——" can't be on the team. We have work to do and don't have time to pamper him. It's time to stand up to him and dampen the departmentalization and inhibitions he causes.

4. To quote Will Rogers: "Everybody is ignorant, only on different subjects." The team members must be of different technical specialties, no more than eight people (and don't cheat here), and from several involved departments.

5. The spokesperson can be a manager, can be a janitor, can be elected, or can be appointed. But—and this rules out most of us—the leader must have remarkable people skills. I mean *outstanding*. The social nurturing of the team is a necessity. Nerds, poker-faces, dinosaur-brains, and bad guys do not qualify. The research shows that the main reason for team failure is the lack of social nurturing. Take no risks here.

6. One hundred percent attendance is required at the 90-minute meetings. These are weekly at first, stretching to biweekly or less often as you get to the experimentation phase.

7. Use a sacred meeting place with lots of board writing space. Meeting in the canteen with people coming in and out, or a jack hammer thundering outside the glass wall dooms you to sure failure.

8. The team members must learn the tools of problem solving (see *SPC for Practitioners: Special Cases and Continuous*

Processes). We seldom use most of the seven or eight standard problem-solving tools, except brainstorming. Correct brainstorming is the major tool to break down the departmental and political barriers. This will take some time because the members will need many days for the concepts to incubate. Never "close the book" on a system problem in one meeting. *Be patient.*

9. If you have to take two- to three-week breaks for training, don't be surprised.

10. Management agrees in advance to implement the team's findings, no questions asked. There should be no cherry picking—the team members never get over this. If there's a maximum amount of money, or an undertaking that is politically impossible, air this out in the beginning. Believe it or not, this total empowerment does not break the bank. The team members form a weighted priority ranking—50 percent based on cost and 50 percent from perceived, gut-feel goodness.

11. A team may meet 20-30 times. The first 10-15 may be unstructured as the members creatively and openly discuss the issues. Being an engineer, I had a difficult time with this confusion in the beginning. I wanted structure and action items in every meeting. I learned that creativity doesn't work that way. Action items eventually come. Again, be patient.

12. Let one member keep informal notes. Do not allow him to maintain formal minutes for management. Creativity does not work that way. Make no exceptions.

13. There can be no routine reporting at business meetings. If you fall into this trap, you will spend all of your time getting ready for meetings to impress the boss.

14. Members can gripe about problems; but sooner or later, you have to get down to talking about solutions.

15. Beware if it looks too easy, or if things are progressing too fast.

Is this different? You bet it is! That's why it works. Don't compromise. Management and the team members must memorize these fifteen items. The novelty of all this is unsettling, so it is good to be able to refer back to the textbook.

An additional point: Teams wane about one-third into their life. You will figure out a way to rekindle the spirits. Refer back to this last paragraph so that, at least, the members will know that they are typical. Good luck!

APPENDIX B

DEMING'S "FOURTEEN POINTS"

1. Create constancy of purpose through improvement of product and service, with the goal being to stay in business.

2. Upper management must learn the new philosophy, use it, and not delegate the responsibility to someone else.

3. Build quality into the products and services to make after-the-fact inspection unnecessary.

4. Use fewer vendors—preferably one. Base selections on quality and service, as well as price. Eliminate low-cost bidder purchasing policies.

5. Expect measurable improvements in quality and productivity, but not through numerical goals.

6. Do not let on-the-job training be the major source for learning by the new-hires.

7. Supervise by creating a productive environment, not by using manipulative gimmicks.

8. Outlaw the use of fear.

9. Take all the steps necessary to remove the barriers among departments.

10. Do not hang up banners asking people to work harder.

11 a. Do not use piece rates or production quotas.
11 b. Do not use management by the numbers.

12a. Remove all barriers to pride of workmanship.
12b. Do not use performance evaluations that rank people.

13. Institute a rigorous program of education and self-improvement.

14. Find a way to get all employees involved.

DEMING'S "DEADLY DISEASES"

1. Lack of constancy of purpose—treating every quarter as the entire future.

2. Too much emphasis on short-term profits.

3. Performance evaluations that pit employees against each other.

4. Myth of the universal manager.

5. After-the-fact management by looking only at the visible figures. Not understanding the importance of the unknown and unknowables.

Ones peculiar to the U.S. and beyond the scope of this or Deming's book:

6. Out-of-control medical expenses.

7. Too many lawsuits.

References

Deming, W. Edwards. *Out of the Crisis*. Cambridge: Massachusetts Institute of Technology, Center for Advanced Engineering Study, 1982.

Fellers, Gary. *Personal Agendas*. Forthcoming.
This book contains the Deming story in a novel. There is a special emphasis on enhancing intuition and creativity. Great for your spouse to see "what you have to put up with at work."

———. *SPC for Practitioners: Special Cases and Continuous Processes*. Milwaukee: ASQC Quality Press, 1991.
This is a source for learning the technical aspects of control charts. You may order this from the American Society for Quality Control by calling 1-800-248-1946.

Givens, Charles J. *SuperSelf*. New York: Simon & Schuster, 1993.

SPC-TQM for Administrations Staff and Fellers, Gary. *The Deming Vision*. Milwaukee: ASQC Quality Press, 1992.
This is a good source for learning how to run the interdepartmental teams, or to grasp the more quantitative approach to Deming's ideas. This is a must for Deming facilitators. To order, contact the American Society for Quality Control at 1-800-248-1946.

I will gladly talk to you on the phone about this subject:

Dr. Gary Fellers
200 Nottingham Way
Anderson, SC 29621
803-231-9855 (phone and fax)